HOW TO CHOOSE
THE
BEST SCHOOL
FOR YOUR CHILD

HOW TO CHOOSE

THE

BEST SCHOOL

FOR YOUR CHILD

BUD HOWLETT

Gulf Publishing Company
Houston, Texas

How to Choose the Best School for Your Child

All photographs, except where noted, by Bud Howlett.

Gulf Publishing Company
Book Division
P.O. Box 2608, Houston, Texas 77252-2608

Library of Congress Cataloging-in-Publication Data

Howlett, Bud.
    How to choose the best school for your child: the long-awaited
solution to the dilemma of finding the right school / Bud Howlett.
        p.   cm.
    Includes bibliographical references (p.) and index.
    ISBN 0-87201-217-4
    1. School, Choice of—United States. 2. Education—United
States—Evaluation.   3. Education—United States—Aims and
objectives. 4. Education—United States—Parent
participation. I. Title.
LB1027.9H69   1991
371—dc20   90-24844
                                                          CIP

10   9   8   7   6   5   4   3   2   1

Dedication

This book is dedicated to my wife, Marsha, who was for many years a school secretary. She understands children. She understands teachers. She understands parents. Above all, she understands principals . . . particularly the one she married! Her many ideas and suggestions, her guidance, and her excellent skill in editing have been invaluable.

Most important, she has given me the time to complete my work. Marsha's loving encouragement has provided the motivation over the years to bring this manuscript to fruition.

Contents

Acknowledgments x

Foreword xi

Introduction xiii

1. How Schools Have Changed 1

Back to the Basics. Catalysts for Change.
Changes Can Be Beneficial. What's Ahead.

2. Understanding Differences in Schools . . 16

The Three Types of Schools. Factors in
Choosing Public vs. Private Education.
Considerations in Choosing Schools.
Differences in Educational Philosophies and
Organizations.

3. Looking at Your Child 36

Parents as Educators. Evaluating Your Child. How Children Learn. Children with Special Needs. Children's Personalities.

4. What Kind of Person You Want Your Child to Be 55

Characteristics Children Learn in Effective Schools.

5. What We Know About Learning . . . 64

Developmental Factors. Psychological Information. The Learning Process. Teaching Methodology.

6. Elements of Effective Schools 81

Clear School Mission or Purpose. Strong Administrative Leadership. Emphasis on Academic Achievement. Quality Instructional Staff. Variety of Instructional Strategies. High Expectations. Safe and Orderly Environment. Protection of Instructional Time. Monitoring and Recognizing Student Progress. Positive Home-School Relationships. Positive School Climate.

7. Additional Important Considerations . . 102

Test Results. Financial Support. Physical Plant. Statement of Policies. Other Factors to Consider.

8. **The Effective Teacher** 116
Identifying the Effective Teacher.

9. **How to Gather Information** 124
Written Information. Visiting the School.

10. **The Parent's Role** 136
What You Can Do.

11. **After You Choose Your Child's School** 148

Appendix A: Effective Schools Checklist 151

Appendix B: Growth and Learning Expectations 155

Growth Characteristics of School-Age Children. Grade Level Expectancies.

Appendix C: Selected References for Parents 205

Glossary of Selected Educational Terms . . 211

Index 217

Acknowledgments

Ken Cooper, former principal and administrator in the Pomona Unified School District, who taught me so much about being a principal.

Dr. Don Leisey, former Superintendent of San Rafael City Schools and former Director of Merryhill Country Schools, who has given me assistance from the private school sector.

Dr. Keith Beery, an inspirational educator, for his continued help, encouragement, and guidance in writing this manuscript.

Foreword

Every parent needs to read this extremely important book!

In *How to Choose the Best School for Your Child*, Bud Howlett is able to share with parents the expertise he has gained from thirty-five years as an outstanding teacher and principal. He shows parents how to recognize those elements that will make a difference in their own child's education.

Bud Howlett is an educator who not only understands what makes excellent education tick, he *does* it and teaches others how to do it very effectively. Most important, he helps parents learn how to recognize a quality education.

Although the students in Bud's school come from an extremely wide socioeconomic range, they progress beautifully — academically, socially, and personally, — as they live and learn in the school environment he fosters. Students and parents alike love this wonderful place called school.

It has been my privilege to work, for nearly three decades, with many fine educators and school systems throughout the United States. Bud Howlett is a *great* educator, one of the best I've known. Because he is so outstanding, I have made it a practice to drop in on Bud's school when he doesn't expect me, so I can learn and enjoy some more from him about what *excellent* education is all about — in action. In this book, Bud passes this wisdom along to parents.

You are in for a rare treat — great wisdom couched in everyday language — from a man who knows and who cares deeply about you and the education of your children.

Keith E. Beery, Ph.D.
Director, Institute for Independent Education Research
Director, Interstate Synergy

Introduction

No one would think about making an investment of $60,000 without some expert advice. Today a parent invests about that amount in the education of each of their children who complete high school [1]. In some cases this money will be paid directly to the school; in the case of public school, it will be paid indirectly, in the form of taxes. In some states and private schools, the cost can be twice this amount. It does not even include investments that parents make in special supplies, uniforms, equipment, or, in the case of boarding schools, room and board. Choosing a child's school wisely, then, makes good financial sense (Figure I-1).

The importance of the child's early educational experience in school cannot be underestimated. It sets the tone and forms the attitudes that will affect the child's learning for many years, perhaps throughout her/his life. Choosing a child's school wisely, then, makes good *educational* sense.

What kinds of choices are available to parents when selecting their child's school? More than most would suspect. The parent who plans to send a child to private school, of course, is only limited by the availability of schools in

Figure I-1. When a child enters kindergarten, the parents have just begun to make an investment in her/his education that will total more than $60,000 over the next thirteen years.

the area (Figure I-2). On the other hand, the parent who plans to send a child to public school may have more options than are readily apparent. Many schools have developed alternative educational programs and every state has schools or districts that give some kind of option to parents [2].

Some school systems offer total self-selection, while others have a policy of open enrollment, which means a child may attend any school, in or out of his neighborhood, providing there is space. Some states have legislation that allows students to attend in a district other than in the area of residence. The magnet school concept has provided parents with nearly unlimited options in selecting schools with specialized programs. Many states are considering offering "parental choice" to the tax-paying public. Many districts offer "second-chance" plans for students who have not been

Figure I-2. The private, independent school is one of the options open to parents.

successful in traditional educational settings. Even within a school, there will be options if the school is large enough to have more than one class at each grade level. Some schools offer a variety of educational plans at individual school sites.

Former U.S. Secretary of Education, Lauro F. Cavazos urged ". . . parents must be involved in helping their children learn and in selecting a quality education matched to their children's needs." [3] Parents, too, voiced their approval of the right to choose their child's public school in the 1989 Gallup Poll [4]. Nearly twice as many (60%) approved choosing their child's public school as opposed the idea (31%).

Parents having a say in their child's education is an altogether reasonable concept (Figure I-3). No one knows

Figure I-3. Choosing a child's school is one of the most important decisions that a parent can make.

the individual child better than the parent. Consider, also, that the parent is the child's first and most influential teacher. The child's personality and much of what will be learned in life will have been taught before formal schooling begins.

The question, then, is not, "Should parents have a say in the selection of their child's school?" but rather, *"How can a parent choose the educational plan which will result in maximum growth for the child?"*

Parents often select a school on the advice of a friend or with the help of information which may not be too reliable. A real estate salesperson, who wants to sell a house, may volunteer information about the local school. Parents may also select a school on the basis of, "When I was a kid, what I needed was . . ." Others may survey the comparative test scores published by some states and assume that the school with the highest test scores is the "best" school. In reality, all of these methods may be ineffective, unproductive, or misleading. However, parents can learn to make effective choices.

We are now in a particularly significant era of education in America because a reform movement has enveloped the educational arena. *A Nation at Risk* seemed to mobilize the nation when the authors proclaimed: "If an unfriendly foreign power had attempted to impose on America the mediocre educational performance that exists today, we might well have viewed it as an act of war." [5] Parents, educators, and legislators have joined together to improve educational opportunities for our children. Responding to a demand for definitive data, we have seen a growing body of meaningful educational research during the last ten to fifteen years (see Chapter 6). The tools to effectively analyze education now exist. We can identify factors that make an effective school, and we can isolate those factors that directly influence learning in or out of schools.

This book will, in down-to-earth language, help you:

- understand the workings of schools and educational systems
- look at a variety of educational plans with their sometimes changing and misleading names
- compare one school with another, one plan with another, one system with another
- compare public schools with private schools
- use the simplified "Effective Schools Checklist" to determine the quality of a school's program
- spot the effective teacher
- determine the importance of the principal and understand what makes for effective educational leadership

- perceive your child's needs in relation to learning
- define the role that you, the parent, play in the education of your child.

How to Choose the Best School for Your Child is not a book advocating public schools, nor does it suggest private schools are an educational panacea. This book describes what constitutes quality education. It provides a long-awaited solution to helping you, as a parent, make wise educational choices for your children.

1. According to data reported by the National Education Association, "The nation's public schools spent an average of $4,890 per pupil in 1989-90 . . ." Projected from kindergarten through grade twelve totals $63,570. *Education Week.* Washington, D.C.: October 3, 1990, pp. 2.
2. Nathan, J. *Progress, Problems, and Prospects of State Educational Choice Plans.* Washington, D.C., U.S. Department of Education, July 1989.
3. Cavazos, L. *Educating Our Children: Parents & Schools Together.* Washington, D.C.: U.S. Government Printing Office, 1989, pp. i.
4. Gallup, A. and Elam, S. "The 21st Annual Gallup Poll of the Public's Attitudes Toward the Public Schools." *Phi Delta Kappan,* Bloomington, IN, September 1989.
5. *A Nation At Risk.* Washington, D.C.: U.S. Government Printing Office, 1983, pp. 5.

CHAPTER 1

How Schools Have Changed

Visiting a classroom today provides an experience that is, in all likelihood, quite different from when you went to school. It has probably been a long time since you sat in Miss Rudrum's fifth-grade class, and you may have forgotten what it was like. Not only have you forgotten what the classroom was like, but you may have also forgotten what you were like, and what Sally, who sat in front of you, or Archie, who sat beside you, was like. It's not only that time has dimmed the memory of the experience, but schools have changed, too.

Are there those among you who remember ink wells? Probably not unless you are enrolling your grandchild in school. Remember how the chairs were all bolted down? Recall the hickory switch or the ruler on the knuckles? Some of us even go back to the stove in the classroom and real slate (nothing has ever worked as well) on the chalkboards. Most things have changed for the better, but not everything. The organization of the classroom, the content of the curriculum, and the maturity of children have all changed (Figure 1-1).

Back to the Basics

What was once described as the "open classroom" has lost its appeal, and the pendulum has swung back to more direct instruction on the part of the teacher. There is greater adherence to a prescribed curriculum. The need for improved discipline, as highlighted by the Gallup poll [1], has been recognized by parents and educators alike and, generally, school principals are running "tighter ships" than they were during the sixties and seventies.

In response to many studies that have compared American and foreign school systems [2], the school day and year have been lengthened and there is more homeowork.

In an attempt to upgrade the teaching profession, more than half the states have set minimum proficiency standards for those entering the teaching profession. In most states some kind of student proficiency standards have been set at various grade levels as a requirement for graduation.

Catalysts for Change

Education is constantly changing to meet the needs of society. Public education, generally, is directed by local boards of education under some kind of state framework. Private schools are, likewise, directed by boards or, in the case of larger systems, directors. As the thinking of local citizens and educators changes, so do educational programs. These changes are often brought about by parents in the school community.

Figure 1-1. Differences in school buildings are but one indication of the changes that have taken place in American schools.

Equal Opportunity

"Title IX," a federal regulation, has brought about changes in opportunities for the sexes and minorities. Sex and race stereotypes have pretty much disappeared from school curricula. In the days of Dick and Jane, father went off to work and mother stayed at home and washed, sewed, cooked, and taught her daughter to do likewise. Furthermore, Dick and Jane were white, middle class children and so were their friends.

One of the differences you may note when picking up a basal reader today is that the first story may be about a Chinese family, the second story about a mother who is a doctor, and, lo and behold, the third a story about life in a single-parent home! We may not find Grandma and Grandpa in such strong evidence now because of the mobility of young people today.

The curriculum is much more similar now for both boys and girls. Some of the older reference books discuss courses for girls, which included home economics, sewing, cooking, and the like, while boys courses included shop and auto mechanics. Varsity athletics was for boys and cheerleading was for girls. Both sexes now enjoy equal access to the curriculum (Figure 1-2), including most varsity sports.

Demographics

Dramatic changes have taken place in America's schools because of demographic influences. "In the past decade, an unprecedented wave of immigrants—primarily (but not exclusively) from the Pacific Rim nations of Asia, from Mexico, and from Central America—has joined our indigenous [population of] blacks, Anglos, Latinos, Asians, and Native Americans to form one of the most ethnically diverse societies in history." [3]

For example, as Cuban refugees flooded Dade County, Florida, the educational system was forced to change to accommodate the new student clientele. Teacher preparation and in-service training was expanded to include teaching English as a second language. Spanish-speaking teachers were recruited and courses in understanding Hispanic culture were developed to increase the sensitivity of educators. Bilingual programs began to be implemented to meet the

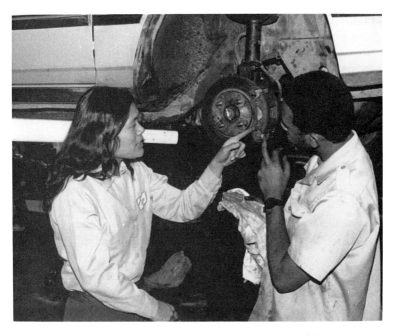

Figure 1-2. Division of students according to sex is a much less common practice today. For instance, it's not unusual to find girls taking auto shop, as well as female instructors for such courses.

needs of non-English speaking students. Increasing multicultural understanding among students became part of the curriculum.

Likewise, California and Texas have changed and expanded their programs dramatically to more effectively teach Hispanic and Vietnamese students (Figure 1-3). Inner-city schools have had to change in an attempt to curb the drop-out problem. With the help of Federal money, funding has been provided for such programs as Head Start.

The impact of immigrants has been felt not only by public schools but, likewise, by private schools. Hispanic students,

Enrollment in California Public Schools

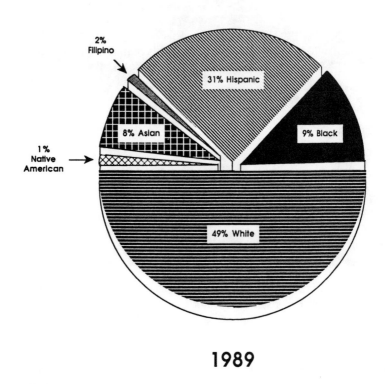

1989

Figure 1-3. In the "immigrant entry states" (New York, Florida, Texas, and California), minorities are rapidly becoming the majority in the public schools. This has already happened in California. Source: California State Department of Education.

who are predominantly Catholic, have had an affect on the parochial school population. Minority enrollment in private schools, as a whole, has climbed to over 10% of the total in the last few years [4].

Scientific Advances

A dramatic example of change in educational emphasis occurred when Sputnik was flung into orbit by the Russians in 1957, beating Americans to space. A cry of alarm went up nationwide, particularly in the fields of math and science. The result was that parents, educators, and legislators began to rethink math and science curricula.

Mathematics is still changing, mainly as a result of comparisons of math scores of students in other nations, particularly in Japan and in European countries. The curriculum is being revised and updated and is generally becoming more advanced. In California, recently, the State Board of Education rejected all mathematics textbook submissions by publishers as not being rigorous enough. Mathematics is only one example of the continual change needed to meet the demands of society.

Educational Writers and Theorists

Educational writers and theorists have been catalysts for change in educational programs as well. Nationally recognized author and philosopher John Dewey [5] created a wide-reaching influence on the establishment of the "learn-by-doing curriculum." The book *Why Johnny Can't Read* [6] resulted in a flood of parents decrying the lack of phonics in teaching reading. It affects parent opinion even today. The opinions of both parents and educators were also affected by Holt's *The Under-Achieving School* [7] and Silberman's *Crisis in the Classroom* [8]. Many district superintendents have had immense impact on their districts. In many cases entire school systems have adopted the thinking of prominent educational leaders and their educational philosophies changed the way children were taught [9].

Society

Other changes in education have been brought about by changes in society. Many people agree that, unfortunately, children in school today must be taught about AIDS, safe sex, adolescent suicide, drug and alcohol abuse, molestation, incest, and what to do if a gunman enters the classroom. As problems are manifested in society, citizens will change the schools in an effort to provide solutions.

Programs such as "Head Start," "Driver Education," English as a Second Language," "Drug Abuse Education," "Computer Assisted Learning," "Compensatory Education," "AIDS Prevention," "Back to Basics," "Team Teaching," and "Year 'Round School" are all programs that have been added as a result of changes in society.

Students' Changing Maturity

What can be most enlightening to adults who are, once again, becoming familiar with the schools are the vast changes that have taken place in the maturity and knowledge of young people today.

Television. Television has opened the adult world to children, and it seems as if nothing is sacred. Recently, I was sitting with a group of fourth- and fifth-grade children over lunch when the discussion at the next table turned to the film on the movie channel the previous evening. The movie happened to be "10," starring Bo Derek. This group of nine- and ten-year-olds had taken in everything on the screen, particularly Miss Derek's physical attributes, and could discuss them with some degree of sophistication. I'm not sure if I was more surprised by their knowledge or by the fact that the movie came on at 11 p.m. and didn't go off until 1:30 in the morning!

With the advent of television has come a sexual awareness among even the very young. Their interaction with each other is on a much more grown-up level and begins earlier than their predecessors. Unfortunately, children have been plunged into an adult world for which they are not emotionally ready. This is bound to happen given the amount of time children spend watching television today—between twenty-five and fifty hours per week [10] (See Figure 1-4).

Sometimes well-meaning parents can do too much for their children. Everything is organized. Many children are

Figure 1-4. The average child in the United States watches between 25 and 50 hours of television per week.

expected to play Little League, Youth Soccer, Bobby Sox, or Pop Warner football, or they're expected to go to drama class, supervised recreation, ballet, music lessons, or tutoring. There is nothing wrong with any of these activities but when they are entirely supervised by adults, children do not learn about independent activities. As a result, instead of playing among themselves children avail themselves of television.

What is missing is children getting together in the neighborhood and organizing a game of kick-the-can or playing "movies-up." It is not the games being played that are important but how children play them. It is important for children to interact with each other, to learn neighborhood leadership, to plan projects and build tree houses—in general, to do things for themselves. Television requires no interaction, either with the set or among those watching. Likewise, many of the games we, as parents, organize for children, may restrict their initiative. As a result, in the classroom we find more of a "What do I do next, Teacher?" attitude than was found in the past.

Drugs and Alcohol. Much of the classic literature about child growth and development discusses children in eighth grade or high school becoming aware of drugs, cigarettes, and alcohol. Not today! We can talk with elementary school children about cocaine and find that their knowledge and vocabulary are quite sophisticated. Kindergarten children, in some communities, are aware of drug availability and crack (a potent cheap form of cocaine) is a familiar word.

I was recently walking across the school playground with a second grader. As we stood near the fence that bordered on the street, she commented casually, "Mr. Howlett, I smell marijuana." I have no doubt that she did and that she recognized it. The fact that this seven-year-old recognized marijuana illustrates that children today, at a very young age, have exposure to, and familiarity with, drugs. California Attorney General John K. Van de Kamp has stated, ". . . it is a sad and sobering reality that trying drugs is no longer the exception among high school students—it is the norm." [11]

Family Structure

Because of the dramatic increase in two wage-earning- or single-parent households, the need for child care, both before and after school, and preschool care, has exploded. Private schools have been much more responsive than public schools. Private schools and day-care centers have moved in to fulfill this need.

Social factors, including divorce, have also changed the family structure. Many teachers have encountered unexpected grief and created anxiety when asking students to do a family tree because some of the limbs are no longer part of the family and may not even be recognized as relatives. "Fewer than 5 percent of U.S. households now conform to the standard model family of past decades—a working father, mother at home, and two or more school-age children." [12]

Approximately one million children are maltreated, physically or sexually abused, or neglected by their parents each year [13]. "One out of every eight students is estimated to be the child of an alcoholic, and one in every five to be the child of a parent or parenting figure who is abusing alcohol or other drugs." [14]

"Today there is more trouble for children and less time for innocence than in recent generations. The problem is not so much that children have changed. The world has changed." [15] The school, of necessity, will respond to these changing patterns in society.

What's Ahead?

Schools, and particularly methods of instruction, will continue to change. Are there any noticeable trends of which parents should be aware? The tendency toward more active learning (see Chapter 2), which places more emphasis on problem solving and creative thinking, seems to be gaining momentum. It is fueled by the infusion of interactive technology, mostly the personal computer, into the classroom (Figure 1-5). Computers are seen as tools to solve problems, store and retrieve data, test hypotheses, facilitate the writing process through word processing, communicate with others, produce graphics, and assist teachers with their many tasks.

There will be differences in the classroom of the future. The role of the teacher will change from the purveyor of information to a facilitator of learning. This means less of the read/lecture and test/recite methods of instruction in favor of emphasis on creating a situation in which students interact with and learn from all resources in their learning environment. These resources may include, in addition to the teacher and the textbook, field experiences, videotapes, laser discs, telecommunications, and computers.

The appearance of the classroom will be altered, as it will have to be configured to utilize technology. There will also need to be space for laser disc equipment, printers, and telecommunications facilities, which will enable learning outside the classroom.

Figure 1-5. A variety of instructional strategies and the use of technology will enable a good teacher to be more effective. (Photo: Stuart Lirette)

It will be noisier. Students will work together more on cooperative projects. The computer creates student socialization because students constantly interact and help each other problem solve. Students working together will be the rule rather than the exception. There will be increased recognition that other students are great sources of learning, which will foster the cooperative learning concept (see Glossary).

This trend may be slow to develop. The cost of equipment is a problem that will take time to solve. Currently, most educators are not trained to utilize available technology. Nor will teachers readily give up their present role for unfamiliar instructional methodologies. Future teachers, I am sure, will more fully realize the promising role of technology in education and utilize it to improve the process of instruction.

Changes Can Be Beneficial

Don't be threatened by change in schools. As a matter of fact, one of the questions that I would encourage parents to ask in looking at a school is "How has this school changed in the last ten years?" If it hasn't changed, that could be a sign of trouble. Bear in mind that changes in education are a result of both educators and parents trying, for the most part, to improve your child's education. Consider that education is dynamic and constantly changing to keep up with society. Make sure that whatever information you gather about a school is current.

Indeed, schools have changed, teaching methods have changed, and children have changed!

References

1. Gallup, A. and Clark, D., "The 19th Annual Gallup Poll of the Public's Attitude toward the Public Schools," *Phi Delta Kappan*. September, 1987.
2. *A Nation At Risk*. Washington, DC: U.S. Government Printing Office, 1983, pp. 8-10.
3. Olsen, L. *Crossing the Schoolhouse Border: Immigrant Children In California*. San Francisco: California Tomorrow Policy Research Report, 1988.
4. *Private Schools of the United States*. Shelton, CT: Market Data Retrieval, 1985-6.
5. Dewey, J. *Philosophy of Education*. Totowa, NJ: Little, Adams & Co., 1975.

6. Flesch, R. *Why Johnny Can't Read*. New York, NY: Harper & Bros., 1955.

7. Holt, J. *The Under-Achieving School*. New York, NY: Ditman Publishing Corporation, 1969.

8. Silberman, C. *Crisis in the Classroom*. New York, NY: Random House, 1970.

9. Goulet, R. *Educational Change: The Reality and the Promise*. New York, NY: Citation Press, 1968.

10. Winn, M. *The Plug-In Drug*. New York, NY: The Viking Press, 1978.

11. Van de Kamp, J. *Schools and Drugs*. Sacramento, CA: Office of the Attorney General, 1987.

12. "Here They Come, Ready or Not," California State Department of Education, *Education Week*. May 14, 1986.

13. Broadhurst, D. *The Educator's Role in the Prevention and Treatment of Child Abuse and Neglect*. U.S. Department of Health and Human Services, Washington, DC: Kirschner Associates, Inc., 1984.

14. Cox, B, and Morehouse, E. "The Role of Pupil Personnel Services Staff with Children of Alcoholics," *It's Elementary: Meeting the Needs of High-Risk Youth in the School Setting*. South Laguna, CA: The National Association for Children of Alcoholics, 1989.

15. Morrow, L. "Through the Eyes of Children," *Time Magazine*. August, 1988, pp. 32.

CHAPTER 2

Understanding Differences in Schools

There are several factors that make the comparison of schools difficult. With a little understanding of these factors, however, comprehending differences and making comparisons becomes a simple task. Analyzing what exists and why allows a better understanding of various educational institutions.

The Three Types of Schools

As a parent, you have three basic options regarding the education of your child. You can enroll your child in a public school system. You can select a private school. Or you can elect to not send your child to school and provide for the child's education yourself.

Home-based Schools

The requirements for self-education differ from state to state and there are numerous questions you should ask, including "Do I have the time to provide for the formal education of my child, myself?" This is, however, an option that some parents may want to consider. The best plan is to inform yourself with a comprehensive book such as *The Home School Manual* [1]. Appendix B should be of assistance to you.

Private Schools

Your second option is private school. There have been private schools in America longer than there has been free public education. These schools meet the particular needs of the children they serve. Private schools differ in a variety of ways because, being outside the restrictions of the public school system, they do not have to adhere to many of the state and federal regulations that govern public schools. They are designed to meet the particular needs of their clientele—academically, socially, behaviorally, and/or religiously.

Private schools served more than 5.2 million students in 1985, or about 12% of America's student population. The largest segment of private schools, more than 80%, has some religious affiliation (Figure 2-1) and approximately half of this group is Catholic [2].

In 1985, nearly three-fourths of the 23,862 private schools in this country belonged to the "Council for American Private Education." This is an umbrella organization that represents the 14 private school organizations to which most schools belong. Members must maintain certain

Figure 2-1. The majority of private schools have some religious affiliation.

academic standards to be considered for membership. Another organization that represents private schools is the "National Independent Private Schools Association." (The addresses of both are listed on page 207.)

The number of private schools continues to grow. A significant factor in their growth has been the willingness of many private schools to recognize the need for full-time care of children during the day, due to the increase in the numbers of single-parent and two wage-earner families. Many private schools provide for their students during the parents' entire workday. Public schools have not moved into the child care business as readily.

Likewise, private schools often serve preschool-age children before they are able to enter public school kindergarten. Once enrolled in a system that parents like, children may continue after kindergarten age, having had firsthand experience with the school. This is, undoubtedly, one of the reasons that private school enrollment has increased at the same time that public schools have experienced declining enrollment.

Public Schools

The third option, and the one that most parents will select, is public school. Generally, this alternative is selected because it is provided at public expense and required by state law. However, most parents do not realize that there are choices available, even within the public school system. Instead, they defer to the local school in the area where they live without exploring what is available. This book will help you realize the options that are available within the public school system.

Factors in Choosing Public vs. Private Education

You may wish to investigate the following factors in considering the differences between private and public education:

Admission Requirements. Public schools are obligated to provide a program for any child who wants to enter. Private schools may have various requirements and may cater to a particular population.

Class Size. Class size in a private independent school will generally be smaller. That is one of their attractive features.

Cost. Whereas public education is free, private schools are not. However, some are not terribly expensive. There are religiously affiliated private schools that charge from $500 to $1,000 per year. Others are more expensive.

Day Care or Preschool Programs. Many private schools operate both preschool programs and before and after school care for their students. This can be a real convenience to parents.

Individualized Instruction. Many private schools take pride in tailoring instruction to the needs of the child. With smaller class sizes, this can be a realistic goal.

Leadership. Private schools must provide responsive leadership to their clients or their financial stability suffers. The headmistress or headmaster, the counterpart of the public school principal, is generally selected with great care. Since private schools are directly accountable to the families of students they serve, the leader must maintain the reputation of the school.

Location. A private school, except by coincidence, will not be located in your neighborhood. Transportation may be a factor.

Secular Values. The Constitution separates "church and state" and, therefore, public schools must avoid teaching religious values. Many private schools make religious instruction or the teaching of secular values part of the curriculum.

Teachers. Private school teachers are generally paid quite a bit less than their public school colleagues. This does not mean they are of lesser quality. Many private school teachers like the private school atmosphere. A poor public school teacher is difficult to terminate. Not so in a private school.

Uniforms. Except for special teams or groups, uniforms are not required at public schools. Many private schools do require uniforms.

There are pros and cons to both private and public education. It is important that the school you choose meets your own needs and the needs of your child. Whether you are considering private or public school, the information in this book will assist you in your decision.

Considerations in Choosing Schools

It is important to note that schools differ widely throughout the United States. They reflect a variety of educational philosophies and organizational plans. Why? Because education in America is considered a responsibility of the local community, organization, or group, and schools mirror the philosophy of the parents of the students they serve. Schools, then, may differ as widely as cities, towns, and groups of people vary. They may even differ quite drastically within a single school district because of the student population, the teaching staff, or the principal. Therefore, it is important to obtain information about the particular school you are considering, not the community or the state.

Terminology

Further confusion exists because terminology describing the educational process changes and differs through time and at various places. Students who have "learning disabilities" are described at least twenty different ways throughout the States. Terms such as "unstructured classroom," "phonetic approach to reading," "cooperative learning," "basic education," "readiness for kindergarten," and "networking" may be misleading or confusing. Many of them have been popularized in literature but have never been clearly understood by parents. Set the terminology aside and find out what goes on in the school and classroom.

Grade Structure

Another consideration is the configuration of the grade structure (see Figure 2-2). Schools are organized in many different ways. One of the more common patterns is an elementary school that serves kindergarten through grade five (although often the elementary school will go through grade six). Junior high schools, which serve grades seven and eight and sometimes nine, are losing popularity to middle schools [3], which serve grades six, seven and eight. High school is generally regarded as grades nine through twelve.

Students' Roles

What is important is not the actual way the school you are considering is organized but how the organization affects students. The youngest children in a school are the babies or freshmen and the oldest are the big kids or seniors. The youngest tend to be treated as the youngest and the oldest are treated as the "big brother/sister." The ability of children to live up to what is expected of them is amazing. The result is that the children in the oldest grade will develop

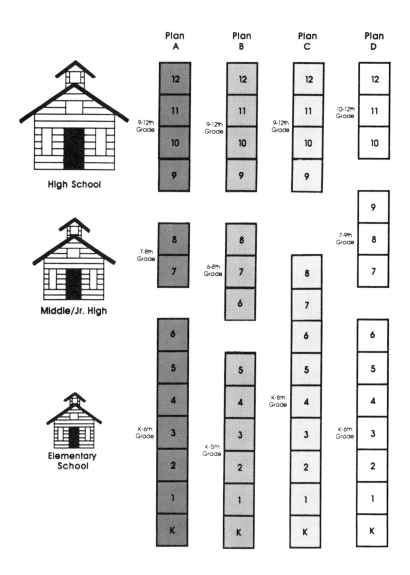

Figure 2-2. Common school grade configurations.

more responsibility, maturity, and leadership because that is what is expected (Figure 2-3). Fifth-grade children in kindergarten through fifth-grade school will be very responsible, more so than if they were fifth graders in a kindergarten through grade-six school. The jobs and responsibilities in the school (everything from safety patrol to serving lunches and being messengers) go to the oldest children and with it comes the opportunity to become more mature individuals. The same is true of the oldest grade in junior high or middle school, and we are all familiar with the nature of high school seniors—they're "boss" of the school!

When students leave elementary school and begin junior high or middle school, the instructional organization changes. Middle and high schools are departmentalized; that is, teaching is conducted along subject matter lines. Rather than one teacher who is responsible for all subjects and 25 students, a teacher is responsible for one subject (say, science or physical education) and 120-150 students. Most middle or junior high schools will ease students into departmentalization, starting with subjects such as physical education, art, music, shop, or science taught by specialists, and with language arts and sometimes math taught by a core or homeroom teacher. Generally, by the end of the middle or junior high school experience, all subjects will be taught by teachers who are specialists, organized by departments.

The important thing to note is that when your child enters middle or junior high school, there are certain responsibilities placed on the student (Figure 2-4). The student is responsible for getting from one class to another several times during the day. The skill of unlocking and getting books in and out of a locker must be mastered. The student

Figure 2-3. The oldest children in the school have numerous opportunities to develop leadership and responsibility.

Figure 2-4. Change that occurs at the middle school or junior high school level requires more responsibility on the part of the student. Changing classes, using lockers, keeping track of assignments, and adapting to a variety of teachers present new challenges.

must be organized enough to get work done when assigned in several different subject areas and get it back to school. The student must be adaptable enough to respond to different personalities and teaching styles, and to make these changes several times during the day. Since there is not just one teacher who knows everything about the student educationally, the child must develop a certain amount of independence and be able to ask for help when she/he needs it.

Differences in Educational Philosophies and Organizations

Now, let's take a look at some of the educational programs and ways that instruction is organized so that we can better understand what educators are talking about. Note that many of the things that educators do, you as a parent do likewise. We just give it a name and organize it because we are dealing with twenty-five or thirty children at a time, whereas you generally work with one child at a time in a family situation.

Active vs. Passive Learning

There are two basic ways that school programs are organized for learning. They are (1) the type in which children explore and find answers for themselves and (2) the type in which the teacher provides information for the children. Infants start to learn by the former method, utilizing trial and error, exploring, and interacting with the environment, using all the senses to experience new things and send new information to the brain. Eventually, as the child matures, the capacity to understand the verbal information of the parent results in the child learning passively, rather than having to experience everything directly. These same models, active and passive learning, are used in school. Consider the diagram showing the Active/Passive Learning Model (Figure 2-5).

Most preschool learning is active. Most high school education is passive. The elementary schools fall somewhere in between, depending on their particular philosophy. These methods are not mutually exclusive but are usually combined in a variety of ways in the classroom. In high-

ACTIVE LEARNING	PASSIVE LEARNING
The child interacts with the environment	The teacher (parent) provides information
Experiences may be random, depending on interest	Learning is structured into sequential steps
Learning is its own reward; satisfaction of the child's curiosity	Rewards are used to promote learning—grades, promotions, praise, etc.
Learning is acquired in many ways, using all the senses	Learning is mostly verbal, either from the teacher (parent) or from books
Emphasis is on problem solving/thinking—may be no right answer	Emphasis is on the right answer, usually from the teacher (parent)
The child learns from a variety of sources	The child is generally dependent on the teacher for learning

Figure 2-5. Active vs. passive learning.

school chemistry, the lecture would be considered passive (Figure 2-6) while the lab experiment might be considered active.

Kindergarten programs depend on a great deal of active or interactive learning—children learning from each other

Figure 2-6. Passive learning entails finding an answer from a book or from the teacher.

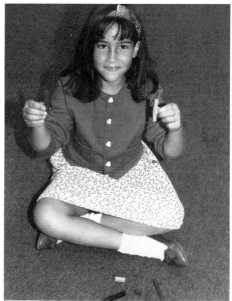

Figure 2-7. Active learning usually results in a student finding an answer for her/himself through discovery. Rods or blocks facilitate this method in mathematics.

and their environment. The beginning of teaching mathematics is generally active (Figure 2-7) or, as we educators also call it, manipulative. The trend in science seems to be toward more active learning or (and here we give it another name) the discovery method.

Students who experience learning difficulties very often have trouble with the passive model and must be taught using more active methods. The critical question here is "How well does a teacher put a particular model into effect?"

Educational Plans

There are a variety of educational plans in schools today. Bear in mind that these plans may be called by different names. There may not be agreement about the use of some of these terms. That's why it is important to know what goes on in the classroom rather than what it is called. Many educational terms are used, misused, and abused. Following are some of the more common education plans you will encounter:

Basics Program. Often called "Back to Basics" or "Essentialist."
- Emphasis is on subject matter, particularly the "3 Rs"
- Curriculum is the same for each student
- Self-contained classroom (one teacher teaches all subjects)
- Strict discipline
- Regular homework
- Letter grades based on set expectancies
- All work completed at a certain level prior to promotion
- Competition with other students deemed healthy
- Considerable memorization, repetition, and drill
- Structured classroom

Traditional Program. Also called "Structured."
- Emphasis on the teacher
- Curriculum is the same for all, but students are grouped for instruction based on ability or achievement level
- Self-contained classroom with one teacher who may share instruction in special subjects such as art, music, or physical education
- Use of traditional graded materials
- Required homework expectancies dependant on age and ability
- Letter grades based on teacher judgment
- Social growth may be emphasized

Continuous Progress. Also called "Ungraded," "Nongraded," or "Individualized."
- Emphasis on individuality and success of the student
- Defined curriculum that children complete at their own rate of ability
- No grade levels; students grouped in class for instruction as needed
- Teaching focused on individual needs with a wide variety of teaching materials
- Regular evaluation, remediation, and reporting to parents
- Promotion occurs when pupil is judged ready for the next level or division
- No particular classroom arrangement
- Diversity is encouraged

Open Classroom. Also called "Unstructured," which refers to flexible scheduling of activities.
- Emphasis is on the child's interest
- Children move at their own rate of speed
- Multiage grouping in classrooms (Figure 2-8)

Figure 2-8. Grouping younger and older children, as well as cross-age learning, may be quite common in open classrooms.

- Exploratory behavior is encouraged, building on child's natural curiosity
- Success oriented
- May be team taught, with more than one teacher
- Wide variety of learning materials—rich learning environment
- Decision-making skills are encouraged
- Children learn from each other—peer teaching
- Verbal abstraction follows direct experience
- Grades not emphasized
- No "sacred" body of knowledge

Developmental Concept. Also known as "Contract Learning," "Cooperative Plan," or "Freeschool."
- Emphasis on personal and social development
- Child is responsible for own learning, sometimes using a contract
- Very much experience oriented in and out of school; learn by doing
- Education is open ended; child can advance as far as he/she is able
- Child learns about citizenship, decision making, creative thinking
- Program based on interest and ability of students
- All learning modes are emphasized
- Teachers, paraprofessionals, parents, and peers are all part of the learning process
- School schedule or course may be flexible
- No promotion or grades, continual evaluation

Montessori Program. Developed by Maria Montessori [4] in Switzerland and sometimes borrowed in part by other plans, particularly nursery schools and magnet-school programs.
- Ordered sequence of multisensory materials, often self-correcting
- Students grouped in multiage developmental groups
- Emphasis on interaction with the environment
- Curriculum geared to child growth and development, social and emotional growth
- Freedom of movement is encouraged
- Children learn "how to learn" skills
- No formal schedule; blocks of time utilized
- Motor skills, sensory integration, and movement development are important

- Respect for individuality is encouraged
- All modes of learning are encouraged

Year-Round School. Also called "45/15 Option" or similar names that designate instructional time blocks.
- Emphasis is on time organization rather than on a particular educational plan
- Could embody any of the preceding plans
- Students attend nine weeks and are off three (or some similar time organization)
- Eliminates three-month summer vacation
- Learning is more continuous
- More time for periodic evaluation
- Less "summer learning dropoff" from long vacations

Team Teaching. Often confused with departmentalization, a process of dividing the curriculum by the subject matter.
- Classroom is taught by more than one teacher
- Total class is larger than normal
- Teachers share responsibility for students, including teaching, evaluating, conferencing, and grading
- Teachers plan curriculum together
- Grouping of children within class is flexible
- Teachers build on their own strengths
- Generally quite activity-oriented
- Noise level may be higher because of class size

Magnet Concept. May include elements of one or more of the plans listed above.
- Parents are given choice if they want their child to attend a particular program
- May refer to a school or a department or program within the school

- Emphasis is on quality program in a particular area or areas, i.e., computers, music, language, basic skills education
- Designed to draw students (hence the term "magnet") from various parts of a district or city because of superiority of a program
- Originally conceived to achieve integration within a system

These are some of the educational plans currently in practice in the United States. Most schools draw something from these different plans at various grade levels. From school to school and from classroom to classroom the teaching philosophy will differ. Remember, whatever the plan is called, take a close look to see how it is put into practice and what actually goes on. Regardless of the educational organizational plan, observe how the teacher uses it and how students respond.

References

1. Wade, T. *The Home School Manual.* Auburn, CA: Gazelle Publications, 1986.
2. *Private Schools of the United States.* Shelton, CT: Market Data Retrieval, 1985-6.
3. Fenwick, J. *The Middle School Years.* San Diego, CA: Fenwick Associations, 1986.
4. Montessori, M. *Childhood Education.* Translated by A. M. Joosten, Chicago: H. Regnery, 1974.

CHAPTER 3

Looking
at Your Child

In order to decide that a school is right for your child, you must first take a look at your own child in relation to that school. Try to take an objective look at your youngster and separate her/his needs from your personal philosophy and feelings about education. Many of your feelings are based on your own educational experience— what worked and what didn't with you. That may not be a valid frame of reference for your child.

For example, Miss Rudrum was my fifth-grade teacher at Cervany School in Detroit. She was a taskmistress! We learned to memorize the forty-eight states the first two weeks of school so that we could spit them back without hesitation. I still can, for that matter—Maine, New Hampshire, Vermont, Massachusetts, Rhode Island, Connecticut . . .

But, before I decide, as a parent, that a good teacher is one who makes students memorize the states, I need to put the experience in the proper context. This was a good experience for me because it let me know who was in charge and what I was supposed to do. But I'm not too sure how valid devoting time to memorizing the states is today when I can pull a printed list off a floppy disk, sorted in any way I like. Perhaps time devoted to learning how to operate a computer would be more productive than memorization in our technological society. An important point to remember: Don't assume what was a good educational experience in "your day" is as valid today. Technology and society have made too many significant changes.

There was something else in that experience which stood out. I remembered how some of the kids in my classroom at Cervany School never did memorize the states. "Dummies! What's wrong with them?" I thought. Having been involved in education for many years, now I know. There are some children who cannot perform this kind of task successfully no matter what the teacher threatens. They're not dumb, but they do have a deficiency in the learning process that makes storage and retrieval of sequential data very difficult or impossible. A second point to remember: Don't assume what is good for some kids is good for all kids, let alone your child.

How valid is your opinion as a basis for evaluating your own child? Excellent! Judy McKnight, writing in *Education Week* [1] put it well when she said, "Parents are experts on their children. We have known them longer and we know them better than anyone else. We are their first and most important teachers."

Parents as Educators

From birth to the age of five, nearly everything your child learned was learned from you or, at least, you provided the environment that enabled learning to take place (Figure 3-1). You taught the child to walk, to talk, to look, to listen, to interact with others, to take responsibility, to understand her/his family, to respond to her/his environment, to perform physical tasks, to have feelings for other beings, and to learn from everything else that exists in his world. You have, in effect, not only set the stage for learning but you have begun the process of education and developed the attitudes that will facilitate or impede the learning process when your child enters school. Former Secretary of Education, Lauro Cavazos, emphasized, "Parents play a crucial role in providing their children with the values and

Figure 3-1. The parent is the child's first and most important teacher. It is at home that the learning process is begun and supported.

skills which are essential to success in school and in later life." [2] Do not underestimate your role as a teacher. No teacher will ever be more important than you!

Your tools, as a parent, differ somewhat from the tools of the teacher. You have provided a natural habitat of playpens, diaper pails, bottles, cribs, rattles, toys, carpets, backyards, grandmas, puppies and, alas, the television set. Upon entering school, the habitat will change and a new set of artifacts will appear. The child will be submersed in lunchboxes, milk money, clothing labels, notices home, books, crayons, and paste, and a third party will enter the child's life—the teacher. This teacher will carry on and supplement, but not supplant, the job you have begun and will continue. Look at education in terms of a partnership and look at school in terms of what it can provide that you can't.

Evaluating Your Child

The only problem is that you must learn to become objective in looking at your child. There are several ways to develop objectivity. Consider her/his level of ability to do school work. Explore the particular style utilized in learning. See if the child has any special needs which need to be taken into account in her/his education. Take a look at her/his unique personality and consider what the child needs to facilitate her/his personal growth. These are not all of the aspects of a child's development to consider in planning an education, but they are some of the most crucial.

What is the ability level of your child? This is a difficult question for most parents to answer because it has, at least partially, to do with intelligence and we are not particularly objective in evaluating our own children. Furthermore, parents do not usually have a sufficient basis for comparison in order to know where their child ranks. You may be puzzled at times as your child has grown by the observation that performance of some tasks is very easy while others are more difficult. What this should say to you is that ability in all areas is not equal.

Standardized Tests

Ability is tested using any one of several standardized I.Q. tests. This is a "norm referenced" test, or one in which a student's score is compared to an average score of a sampling of many scores, usually a nationwide sample (Figure 3-2). The I.Q. score tells where a child ranks compared with other children if 100 is the average score.

The I.Q. test does not enjoy the popularity it once held because it is heavily weighted toward knowledge of the "standard" English vocabulary, and it is not a fair test for the many culturally diverse groups in our country. It is useful, however, to determine expectations we have for children who score significantly above or below average.

This observation provides a basis for understanding that intelligence has two basic components: cognitive ability (or the capacity to think and use knowledge) and performance (or the capacity to do physical tasks). The cognitive aspect is more important to most school tasks because this trait usually results in rapid development of vocabulary and reading skills. Performance, on the other hand, is a measure of the ability to successfully participate in the physical activities that the child is expected to perform. Good performance ability generally results in good writing skills, the ability to manipulate objects, talent in physical education, and the ability to solve puzzle-type problems.

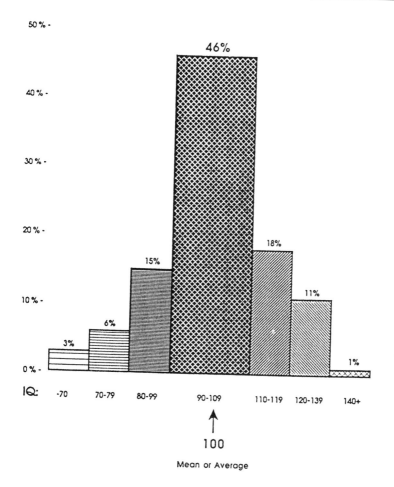

Figure 3-2. Distribution of I.Q. scores in the United States.

Comparing Your Child to Others

Now, how do you assess your child's ability? You compare with other children. If "average" is the midpoint in a normal distribution of children, by definition half of all children are above avarage and half are below average. As a school principal, however, I have found very few parents who have told me, "My child is below average in intelligence."

But if half of all people are below average intelligence, can it be that bad? Not at all. Without question, many of the world's greats could have been categorized this way. If a child is bright, no parent has trouble recognizing this fact and can set certain expectations. If a child has less-than-average ability, then expectations must be different and in line with what the child is able to do. Otherwise, it will be a life of frustration for both parent and child. As a child progresses through school, the child's ability level becomes more apparent.

Much research now indicates that intelligence is not the most important factor to school success. "High academic achievers are not necessarily born 'smarter' than others, nor do people born with extraordinary abilities necessarily become highly accomplished individuals." [3] There are many personality traits that affect success. Hard work and self-discipline play a role. Perhaps the most important trait is self-concept—how the child feels about her/himself can be a more important determiner of school success than native intelligence (Figure 3-3). What is important is that the educational program takes into account children of various levels of intelligence and ability and provides adequate stimulation for children similar to yours.

Here's a hypothetical example of a problem that could occur if you are not objective about your child's ability to do school work: You have a child of "average" ability. You have chosen Lawndale Elementary School because their test scores are the highest in town. The average student at Lawndale is achieving two years above grade level. The

Figure 3-3. How the student views her/himself can be more important in determining school success than native intelligence.

curriculum reflects this achievement level. Now, where does your child fit in? Will this educational setting provide a real stimulus for your child to become an overachiever or are you creating a frustrating experience for a child who will be at the "bottom of the class"? It depends on how children similar to yours are handled, and this is what you need to determine. A student population with a wide socioeconomic mix is generally favored because, in this situation, we almost always find children of all abilities and schools must respond to this wide variety of abilities in its students. Whatever your child's ability, you want a school to challenge him to the maximum of that ability. You also want that school to make your child feel good about her/his efforts. And remember . . . all children can learn the prescribed curriculum if the time and method of presentation is varied.

How Children Learn

Let's examine the second aspect of your child's unique capacities, and become more aware of how your child learns. If you have more than one child in your family, you are probably amazed at how different your second child is from the first. Yet, you raised them in the same environment and provided similar experiences. Imagine, then, how children vary in a school, coming from as many different environments as they do. In any classroom, there are no two children who learn things in the same way. Each child has a distinct style of learning that is as individual as her/his personality.

There are, generally speaking, three categories of learning styles, which may be described as *visual* (reading), *aural* (listening), and *kinesthetic* (doing things). The visual learner learns best from seeing things (Figure 3-4). This student will probably be a good reader, readily learn to use a library, and be a whiz at interpreting maps, charts, and graphs.

The aural learner takes in information effectively by hearing what it is she/he must know (Figure 3-5). This student benefits from the lecture method of teaching, talks a lot to friends, and is able to study while there are other sounds in a room. This person may have trouble with maps but be able to listen to and find the way if directions are given aurally.

The third type of learner is kinesthetic or physical (Figure 3-6). This child tends to be very active and wants to pick up and handle everything. She/he may prefer to move while

Figure 3-4.
Visual learners
are usually
good readers
and learn well
from written
material.

Figure 3-5. Aural learners are good listeners and respond well to that which can be heard.

Figure 3-6. Kinesthetic learners are physically active and may handle objects to maximize learning.

reading, or act out a story rather than read it. This student generally gets her/his muscles into work, and takes more time and may even require a period of physical activity to warm up before starting school work.

Recognize that not all children exhibit only one learning style. To some extent, children will exhibit all styles of learning, but one will probably be most dominant. The important thing to realize about learning styles is that children can build on their own strengths and limitations if they are recognized. Frank Riessman, an authority on learning styles, notes, "A pupil can take advantage of the strengths inherent in his style of learning to balance his weaknesses." [4]

For the parent, it is important to note if a school or an educational program recognizes different learning patterns in children and applies different teaching strategies in order to reach them. If a child is a kinesthetic learner, what a disaster to be in an educational setting in which reading and lecturing are the only methods of presentation!

Children with Special Needs

In addition to a consideration of learning styles we want to look at any special needs of the child. "Special needs" is used in its broadest context and refers to everything from handicaps to giftedness. This is where public and private schools differ dramatically. A private school may appeal to any clientele it wishes. A public school, on the other hand, is obliged to provide an appropriate education for all children, regardless of their unique needs.

Giftedness

Giftedness is a quality of high intellectual functioning that requires special educational attention. In addition to outstanding academic ability, it may also refer to talent and potential for creative endeavour. Generally, giftedness is determined by some means of testing. Individual I.Q. tests as the sole means of identification are finding less favor. This is because we know they do not work well with certain kinds of children, particularly with certain cultural groups because the test depends so much on native language and cultural experiences.

Your concern, as a parent, is determining if there is a process of identification and what kind of program is provided. Special groupings, acceleration, and enrichment may be utilized to accommodate the child. What needs to be considered is if the school provides any of the following educational elements that might be advantageous to the child:

- Interactions with peers who are of the same intellectual level, as well as with students who are different
- Pacing of content, complexity, depth, and breadth of study
- Provision of more challenging materials and resources
- Indivualization of some of the school program, including advancement in classes as appropriate
- Inclusion of the teaching of creativity, productive thinking, and use of talents
- Development of self-understanding and guidance

Disabilities

Other special needs that we might consider are manifested in students with handicaps. This term refers to children who have mental, emotional, or physical disabilities that interfere with normal learning. Public Law 94-142 [5] requires that public schools provide specially designed instruction for children whose individual differences are so great that they cannot learn in a regular classroom setting. Bear in mind that a handicap may be mild or severe, may be temporary or permanent, and may occur with other handicaps. All handicapped students may benefit from some kind of intervention or special program.

If you have a child who has a physical disability such as deafness or blindness, or who is mentally retarded or emotionally disturbed, you are certainly aware of this handicap. Parents of children with learning difficulties, however, may not be cognizant of the problem their child is facing in school. They may simply see their child as shy, awkward, easily confused, frustrated, forgetful, hyperactive, or having difficulty following directions or concentrating. Any of these traits could indicate a problem.

What is confusing to parents is that the terms used to describe this program are not consistent. Children with learning difficulties are identified by forty-three different terms throughout the fifty states. "Educationally handicapped," "neurologically handicapped," "brain damaged," "language disabled," and "perceptually disabled" are all terms used to describe the child who has normal intelligence but whose brain does not perceive or process information effectively. For this type of child, learning in the regular classroom is sometimes virtually impossible.

If you have reason to suspect that your child has a handicap—some type of learning disability, for instance—make sure that there is a process for early identification and a program that meets your child's needs (Figure 3-7). Public schools are required to provide these programs; however, what you need to determine in any school is how the program interfaces with the regular educational program because, in placement, your child has a right to "the least restrictive environment." This is a term that means that a student is removed from the regular classroom only as much as is needed to provide remediation. The attitude of the staff toward handicapped children is also an important factor to consider.

Language Differences

One other classification of children with special needs should be mentioned at this point. These are "language-

Figure 3-7. Some students may benefit from special activities designed to remediate weaknesses in certain areas of learning.

minority children" or children who do not speak English, either because they were foreign-born or because they have grown up in a family where English is not spoken. The number of language-minority children in our schools, because of the conflicts in Southeast Asia and Central America, the political situation in Cuba, and economic conditions in Mexico, now far surpasses the number of handicapped children. This is an interesting phenomenon, because what starts out to be a disadvantage to learning can become a distinct asset to the student and, indeed to our nation if the bilingualism of the child is maintained (Figure 3-8).

Figure 3-8. Language-minority students can have a distinct advantage if the primary language is maintained as a second language is learned.

There are certain questions the parent of the language-minority child needs to ask. Does the school provide an ongoing ESL (English as a Second Language) program? Success in an American school, after all, depends upon mastery of the English language. Does the school provide any support in the primary language so that learning in the basic skill areas can continue while the child learns English? Realize that this may not be possible, except for the major languages in a particular community. And, finally, does the school provide instruction in the primary language so that the child is truly bilingual and can use both languages to her/his own and our nation's advantage? "Even as the business community is recognizing the importance of developing language skills in order to complete in the world economy, we are doing very little in the schools to nurture and develop the natural language resources of our children." [6]

How foolish for a child to enter school in this country speaking Spanish and lose the native language only to have to learn it again in high school as a requirement for college! But it happens more than we admit.

Generally, the more language-minority children in a school or community, the stronger the program will be. Resources will be allocated in areas of greater need.

Children's Personalities

A brief look at personality may put some of the other traits of the child into focus. Personality refers to the consistent patterns of behavior: attributes and qualities or conceptions of one's self that differentiate one human being from another and determine who a person really is.

The initial shaping of personality takes place within the family and is quite well developed by the age of two. Don't you remember some kid in kindergarten who was already obnoxious? Remember the one who was a leader right from the beginning? Personality is further developed through contacts with relatives, peers, teachers, and other community agents. The child's personality will, in part, determine how he reacts to the educational setting and help you determine some of the elements you are looking for in a school.

It will be helpful if you, the parent, can look at your child and see some of aspects of his personality that the school can further develop. For instance, if your child has, for some reason or another, not developed an adequate self-concept, you may want to know what a school does to develop this aspect of personality and make students feel good about what they do. If your child tends to be shy and reluctant to make new friends, you may want to see what a school does to develop self-confidence, and how much emphasis is placed on oral language and drama activities. If your child is very dependent and lacks decision-making abilities, you will probably not want to place this child in a classroom where children are expected to be self-directed. In other words, take a look at your child's personality and decide what aspects you feel the school might further develop and then determine what the school offers.

References

1. McKnight, J. "Parents Are 'Experts' on Their Children." *Education Week,* November 29, 1989, pp. 24.
2. Cavazos, L. *Educating Our Children: Parents & Schools Together.* Washington, DC: U.S. Government Printing Office, 1989.

3. *WHAT WORKS: Research About Teaching and Learning.* Washington, DC: United States Department of Education, 1987.
4. Riessman, F. "Styles of Learning." *NEA Journal,* March 1966, pp. 17.
5. *A Parent's Guide to Public Education for the Handicapped.* Arlington, VA: National School Public Relations Association, 1978.
6. Olsen, L. "Crossing the Schoolhouse Border: Immigrant Children In California." *Phi Delta Kappan,* November 1988, pp. 216.

CHAPTER 4

What Kind of Person You Want Your Child To Be

Your own beliefs concerning the personal qualities you feel your child should exhibit upon completion of formal education should be examined. Put another way, you need to answer the question "What, in my opinion, is an educated person?" Unless you look at the finished product, it may be difficult to decide if the means are adequate to accomplish this end.

Teaching personal characteristics is a separate and unique part of the school program and differs from the acquisition of the basic academic skills, which are included in the prescribed curriculum. Furthermore, there are other personal qualities that may be taught more effectively in the home. For instance, honesty and a sense of ethical and moral conviction should be part of the child's upbringing. The school will reinforce these attributes, to be sure, but there are certain attributes that are best taught by example through parenting. Complete agreement as to what personal attitudes an educated person should possess will not be found, nor will total agreement as to which characteristics should be the major responsibility of the school. Each parent needs to decide what she/he is looking for and make that list (Figure 4-1). Some ideas may find general agreement.

Figure 4-1. Parents need to decide what traits, learnings, and attitudes they feel are important for their child to carry into adult life.

Characteristics Children Learn in Effective Schools

The following personal characteristics or viewpoints are generally considered important, and should be a major responsibility of the school. A child that has been taught in an effective school:

Views education as an ongoing process. Knowledge increases and changes, so the educational process must continue. Because a student must function in a changing world, she/he must maintain a positive attitude toward growth throughout life. Introspection must become part of the child's personality. Much of the factual knowledge we have today will be obsolete by the time the child enters the job market. The child needs to know how to learn, develop an inquisitive attitude, and enjoy the learning process.

Considers diversity an asset to society. Because America is one of the most diverse societies in history, it is important that its citizens learn to appreciate and effectively function with diversity. If the experiences of your children prior to entering school are with children similar to themselves, it may be important to learn to interact and appreciate children who are "different." Different is a term used in its broadest sense and it means children who vary in ability, appearance, racial background, economic background, intelligence, belief, or any other unique physical or mental characteristic.

In a multicultural society, an adult finds her/himself interacting with a broad cross-section of people, both at work and socially. There are parents who would agree that the best place to learn to understand and value individual differences is in school. Indeed, having such experiences beginning in kindergarten is the easiest and most natural because children at this age are so open to learning, accepting others, and making unprejudiced judgments. Remember, we learn more from our differences than from our similarities.

Takes responsibility for own behavior. A basic difference between the child entering school and most adults is responsibility. The young person must be supervised in all activities: in play, in work, in study, in eating and sleeping, and in interactions with others (Figure 4-2). As students grow, they take more responsibility for both their own behavior and their learning. Once in the work world, the adult must assume total control. The person who doesn't, of course, will have control imposed externally. In order to learn how to handle responsibility, one must be given responsibility. Inherent in the giving of responsibility is the understanding that mistakes will be made but these will also be part of the learning process.

Relates to others in a positive way. There has been great discussion about the school's role in teaching children to get along with each other. There are those who maintain this skill should be taught in the home. True, it should be taught and modeled in the home but it must also be an integral part of the school curriculum. Positive people-interaction skills can be learned one-to-one, but they must also be learned in dealing with groups. Surveys of reasons for workers losing their jobs always include "inability to get along with others" as a major reason for termination. No matter how a person chooses to spend her/his life, human interaction will play a major role and thus it is an important personal characteristic.

Figure 4-2. No matter how a person chooses to spend her/his life, positive human interaction will play an important role.

Demonstrates active citizenship skills. It goes without saying that in order to maintain a democratic form of government, citizens must be trained to function in that government (Figure 4-3). They must learn what good citizenship entails and why it is important in a democracy. Children must learn to differentiate between what makes a leader and what makes a follower early in life. They learn this lesson quickly when they find out that the kindergarten teacher doesn't have to raise her hand to speak! Further, they must learn why the teacher doesn't have to raise her hand.

Figure 4-3. Active citizenship skills are learned by studying the origin of our nation as well as by interacting with others.

Other citizenship skills are learned early. It isn't long before any classroom will come into disagreement on an issue and resolution will be reached by means of a vote. The importance of compromise is also important. There are few teachers who haven't had the experience of a child sharing a pet, such as a gerbil, and being asked whether it is a boy or girl and not knowing. Invariably, the class will respond, "Let's vote!" They also learn that there are certain things on which we don't vote.

It is important for children to learn when and how to move from the role of follower and step into the leadership role. The responsibility of being a leader and responsibility of being a follower are critical skills. People learn to lead and to follow by being leaders and followers, and school is a natural place to spawn and nurture these skills.

Has a strong sense of self-worth. A child develops a feeling of positive self-concept by perceiving her/himself as liked, acceptable, and capable (Figure 4-4). Children who

Figure 4-4. Students who have opportunities to feel good about themselves and develop self-confidence are more liable to be successful in school and in later life.

feel good about themselves have been successful in their preschool life. In order to keep moving ahead in life and growing academically, one must anticipate that school success is an attainable goal. Increasing evidence indicates that student failures in basic school subjects, as well as lack of motivation and involvement, may be due in large part to unhealthy perceptions of the self and the world. Many students in school have difficulty, not because of lack of intelligence but because they perceive themselves as being unable to do the work.

There is growing recognition of the relationship between a positive self-concept and school success. You will want to see if a school recognizes the importance of self-concept and how it enhances the job you have begun.

Makes decisions rationally. Perhaps one of the greatest differences in schools today and schools several generations ago is the emergence of teaching critical thinking skills. In Miss Rudrum's class, I learned the basics, or else! There wasn't much room for making your own decisions, selecting from options, or problem solving. In fact, anyone who strayed very far from her agenda knew what it felt like to want to crawl under a desk and hide.

Today more than ever, children need to know how to make decisions. Options are presented to children at a very early age. Television and other social phenomena have brought the adult world to childhood. Even in elementary school, children have opportunities to experiment with drugs, sex, alcohol, and a wide range of antisocial activities that can destroy a young life.

The skill that is needed today is the ability to apply the scientific method to problem solving. Children need to be able to define a problem, select options, predict outcomes,

Figure 4-5. Children today need to develop skills in problem solving through the group process.

take a course of action based on valid information and, finally, evaluate their decision. Children need practice in decision-making both at home and in school, and they need the opportunity to make mistakes from which they can learn (Figure 4-5).

In addition to the regular school curriculum, these are some of the personal characteristics that you may want your child to have. Consider others that are important to you and jot them down. When it comes time to compare schools, they will be important.

CHAPTER 5

What We Know About Learning

Evaluation of an educational program or a teacher is often accomplished on the basis of "what seems to be reasonable." Sometimes the outward appearance of the classroom, the personality of the teacher, or how quiet the children are become the major criteria for judging whether or not learning is taking place. These factors may or may not be important in a given classroom at a given time, but there are much better ways to judge an educational program, and that is on the basis of what we know about learning.

Many studies have been conducted by scientists, psychologists, and educators to learn more about how learning takes place. Anyone who has taken introductory psychology will be familiar with the names. Pavlov [1] studied the learning patterns of dogs, and Skinner [2] of rats. Then there was the extensive work of Thorndike [3] who put animals and humans through all sorts of experiments to study learning. Maslow [4] refined our knowledge about motivation. Piaget [5] and Bloom [6] have further refined educational theories. Many more practitioners of psychology, child growth, development, and the learning process have added to our knowledge.

These studies, when applied to human behavior, have given us a great deal of insight about how children learn and have provided a basis for sound teaching. We can also see that some of the procedures and practices of the "good old days" weren't really that educationally sound. We know, for instance, that in order for citizens to function in a democracy, they must have knowledge and practice in democratic skills. The authoritarian schoolroom, like the authoritarian home of an earlier day, is inconsistent with the skills we want children to acquire. If we keep in mind some basic information about how children learn it will give us a much better basis from which to make judgments.

How do I present to you the knowledge obtained from these hundreds of studies of human behavior in this book? I can give you a few guidelines that help many modern educators (and parents). Each one is briefly described, without reference to the many researchers who contributed to that knowledge. Some interpretation from the insights I have developed in my thirty-five years in the field of educating youngsters is made. Generally, however, this information is psychologically sound and widely accepted.

This information is divided into four sections: developmental factors, psychological information, learning processes, and teaching methodology. Contained in each section is information relating to that particular area.

Developmental Factors

Growth

Individuals grow and learn at different rates. Growth is a continuous, steady process and takes more or less time depending upon the individual learner. Growth and learning take place from where a student is, not from an artificial standard.

Health/Nutrition

Some children cannot learn anything until their physical condition is satisfactory. If a child does not have adequate nutrition and rest and has not had physical problems corrected, he will not experience optimum learning. Physical health comes before mental vigor.

Individuality

It is normal for learners to differ in a vast number of ways. Just as students differ in height, weight, and physical appearance, so they will differ in their ability to learn, their rate of learning, and the way they learn.

Parents

The parent is the child's first and most influential teacher. Nothing will have as great an affect on learning as the preparation that is provided at home (Figure 5-1). Parents can have a dramatic affect on their child's oral-language skills, readiness for reading, ability to count and work with numbers, and general attitude toward learning and school.

Figure 5-1. Nothing will affect learning more than the preparation that is provided in the home.

Students develop in terms of all the influences that affect them. Learning takes place not only in school, but also before children enter school and during all the days that students are not in school.

Readiness

Learning cannot occur until the human organism is ready. It must reach the proper level of physiological and psychological maturity for the given task. The level of readiness to read, for example, occurs in most children at about the age of 6 years. Any attempt to force the learner to perform a task for which he is not ready will result in frustration for both the teacher and the learner.

Psychological Information

Acceptance

Accepting a student for whatever she/he is—her/his ideas, feelings, behaviors, and knowledge—provides a safe climate for a student to take risks in learning and begin to evaluate her/himself.

Adjustment

Children are not effective learners until they adjust to school. Children carry any undesirable attitudes or maladjustment developed from difficult home situations (fighting, abuse, mistrust, physical or emotional neglect, etc.) to school. School has to be viewed, by the child, as a safe environment, both physically and psychologically.

Attitude

How a student feels that others perceive him can affect his/her learning. The attitude of other students, parents, and teachers is important.

"Average" Learner

The average student is largely a myth. "Average" is derived from adding all measures or scores and dividing by the number of scores. It is the midpoint on a scale. In reality there may not be anyone at this point. Average simply provides a standard, but virtually all students will either fall above or below the average.

Fear or Tension

When a learner experiences an abundance of fear, it inhibits learning. Anxiety or tension have detrimental effect on learning by blocking incoming information.

Forgetting

The average person retains only a small part of all factual material presented. The brain has a nearly infinite capacity for learning but most facts will be forgotten. However, fundamentals, such as ways to think about problems, study techniques, how to utilize opportunities, and one's own capabilities, will be remembered.

Intelligence

I.Q., or intelligence, is simply one part of mental ability. I.Q. is measured by intelligence tests. Such tests do not measure other important traits such as creativity, initiative, courage, and self-concept. Intelligence has to do with the ability to learn or understand from the experience which has already been gained.

Intelligence is not as important to success in school as was once thought. Hard work, a positive attitude, perseverance, and self-discipline are probably more important to success in learning than innate intelligence. A high I.Q. does not guarantee a high level of learning.

Praise

Generally speaking, praise is a more powerful motivator than reproof or criticism. The praise, however, must be used selectively and in a meaningful context. Put another way, it is best to accentuate the positive.

Self-Concept

There is a positive relationship between self-concept and achievement. Poor self-concept and the inability to learn are often closely related. A negative perception of one's self is probably more significant to the inability to learn than intelligence. A student's attitude toward himself has great impact on his cuccess in school subjects. Underachievers underestimate their own learning ability.

The Learning Process

Cooperation

For most students, cooperation is a more effective stimulus to learning than competition, although both can be effective when mixed in the right proportion. Students who feel that they can compete successfully will do so, but some of those who feel they can't are liable to withdraw. Cooperative learning, on the other hand, poses no threat and is a winning situation for everyone (Figure 5-2).

Learning Styles

People learn in different ways. There are a great many different styles of learning but learning is increased if an

Figure 5-2. Cooperation is often a more effective stimulus to learning than competition.

individual can be helped to expand the range of learning strategies that she/he can apply. Students learn more if they can learn by listening, seeing, and touching and manipulating objects and by using all combinations of the senses.

Memorizing

Memorization is an important part of learning (Figure 5-3). It enables students to recall information that is used in problem solving and critical thinking. Higher levels of thinking do not take place unless the student is able to rapidly recall specific facts or bodies of knowledge. Two

Figure 5-3. Memorization is an important part of learning because problem solving requires the rapid recall of memorized information.

devices help improve the student's ability to memorize: (1) relating new information to that which is already known, and (2) mnemonics or devices that, in an abbreviated way, help remember important facts through the use of numbers, initials, saying, etc. (for example, E, G, B, D, F are remembered as the notes on a scale by saying Every Good Boy Does Fine).

Patterns

Isolated bits of information are not learned well. Neither is this kind of information retained well because it bears no relation to what is already known or to other information that is being learned. We learn facts and skills best when we learn them in a pattern, in relation to other things, or how they are to be used. The term used in psychology is "Gestalt," which refers to the total configuration rather than the parts.

Practice

Learners often need much practice in order to reach mastery. The practice needs to be realistic and related to that which is to be learned. Children learn to read better by reading more, both in and out of school. Math skills, likewise, are improved through practice.

Punishment/Reward

It is more effective for learners to be rewarded for a correct response than to be punished for a wrong one. Because there are so many wrong responses, it is better to select and reward the correct response than it is to punish the learner for a mistake. Instead of telling a child what not to do, teach him what to do.

Repetition

Routine repetition, or repeating something in the same way, is not an effective way to learn. Rather than repetition, a pupil will learn better if: (1) he is interested, (2) he can use it, or (3) it forms some kind of a pattern. Repetition differs from practice in that the function of practice is to learn to do something better or improve.

Structure

Students learn more when the learning process is structured. This includes letting students know what their goal is, identifying how they are going to accomplish it, realizing the limitations of time, presenting organized assignments, assessing or questioning, providing practice, and evaluating the learning experience.

Time on Task

The amount of time spent in academic learning bears a direct relationship to achievement in school. "Academic learning time" refers to the amount of time a student spends engaged in academic tasks of appropriate difficulty with a high rate of success. The length of the school year, the length of the school day, and the length of time devoted to a subject is critical to what is learned.

Tutoring

Tutoring can improve learning for both the student and the learner. The person who is providing the instruction improves her/his knowledge of the subject and the person being tutored improves both her/his knowledge and his attitude.

Teaching Methodology

Assessment

When teachers regularly and frequently assess student progress and provide prompt feedback, student motivation and achievement improve. Assessment provides the basis for the teacher to know how effective her/his teaching is and for the learner to know what is mastered and what is yet to be learned.

Attention

The more attention that is paid to the student—by the teacher, aides, volunteers or parents—the more the student learns.

Expectations

How well students learn and how well they behave is largely determined by what is expected by the teacher. The learning expectations teachers have often become self-fulfilling prophecies. In order for students to behave and learn, a positive expectation must be communicated to them. This is true for an entire class as well as for individual students.

Homework

Homework can increase learning. Well-designed homework (that is, well-prepared and explained homework) is pertinent to what is being studied (Figure 5-4). If it is assigned at the appropriate level and is corrected and returned to the student, it increases and enhances learning.

Lifelike Learning

Teaching should be lifelike. Methods of teaching should be as much as possible like those used in actual living. Simply put, if we can make school experiences more lifelike,

Figure 5-4. Homework can increase learning if it is well prepared and pertinent to what is being studied.

learning is more effective and permanent. For example, if we want children to learn to be leaders, we should give them experience leading in school. Attitudes, habits, and skills for life are best learned when similar experiences are encountered at school (Figure 5-5). Upon leaving school, the parts in life that pupils play are not new to them.

Meaningful Experiences

A person learns more quickly if she/he sees a reason for learning. The learning then has more meaning. If the

Figure 5-5. If teaching uses lifelike experiences, learning is more effective and permanent.

teacher can present information so that a student can see the value of learning, more learning is likely to take place.

Modeling

Students learn more effectively if they can observe the teacher modeling appropriate behavior. Students will sense a discrepancy between what they are taught and the teacher's behavior if it does not match. For example, if teachers are to teach effective listening skills, then they must be good listeners themselves.

Motivation

Students learn better when they are interested in what is being taught. If they perceive information as helpful, interesting, or rewarding or it produces positive and pleasurable experiences, it is more likely to be learned and retained. Not only is the information important, but the way in which it is presented by the teacher is critical.

Recitation

Recitation is a technique that helps students learn and understand what they have read. Recitation means that the learner puts the material in his own words and repeats it in discussion or in writing. Recitation should not be confused with memorization, which is repeating something verbatim.

Study Skills

Learning is most effective when students possess adequate study skills. Study skills include organization of time, loca-

Figure 5-6. Learning is most effective when students have learned the skill of finding information themselves.

tional or reference skills (Figure 5-6), the ability to identify main ideas, and the ability to clarify and put ideas in writing. Study skills are not simply acquired but must be taught.

Success

Success is an important motivator for learning because it increases security and self-confidence. No one can learn well if she/he constantly fails. In order for a student to learn well she/he should be successful at least three-fourths of the time.

References

1. Pavlov, I. *Selected Works.* Translated by S. Belsky, Moscow: Foreign Languages Publishing House, 1955.
2. Skinner, B. *About Behaviorism.* New Yokr, NY: Knopf, 1983.
3. Thorndike, R. and Hagen, P. *Measurement and Evaluation in Psychology and Education.* New York, NY: John Wiley & Sons, 1977.
4. Maslow, A. *Motivation and Personality.* New York, NY: Harper and Row, 1954.
5. Piaget, J. *Origins of Intelligence in Children.* New York, NY: International Universities Press, 1952.
6. Bloom, B. *Stability and Change in Human Characteristics.* New York, NY: John Wiley & Sons, 1964.

CHAPTER 6

Elements of Effective Schools

First, let's decide on the definition of "effectiveness." The studies that have been done on effective schools in the past generally considered effectiveness defined as achievement in the basic skills. The level at which students achieve in reading, language, and math are the indicators.

However, this is a rather narrow definition of an effective school. The high achiever in school may not be a successful citizen in society. Conversely, a student who tests relatively low in school may turn out to be an extremely productive, happy adult. There are too many factors that determine the eventual success of an individual besides grades in basic skills. Achievement tests do not measure self-esteem, happiness, respect for others, committment to ideals, patriotism, etc. Consider some of the pitfalls associated with a totally academic emphasis.

A school in which there are a significant number of language-minority students, for instance, will not be able to compete with an upper-middle class school of all English-speaking students on a test of basic skills. That does not mean one school is more effective than another. The real measure of effectiveness is the end product—the adult who has come through the school.

What we're looking for in the effective school is the maximum academic, emotional, and social growth for your child. At a certain level of development in some children, it may be much more important to pay attention to school climate, self-esteem, and the nurturing attitude of teachers than to academic emphasis. When we consider the nature of children who are entering schools today, this is particularly true. The child who is learning disabled, abused, a product of a recent divorce, a language or racial minority, or who has a very low self-image may need remediation of a non-academic nature first.

The factors that determine effectiveness, even though they use test results in basic skill areas as the major factor, are nevertheless viable in determining a good learning environment. The importance placed on this factor will need to be evaluated by you, the parent, knowing what the needs of your child are. Test results in the basic skill areas need interpretation. The importance of test results are considered in Chapter 7.

During the last two decades, extensive new research has more clearly identified the factors that determine the effectiveness of a school. We can now pretty well pinpoint those factors that contribute to a good learning environment.

This body of knowledge has developed from studies conducted for the most part, by various state and national organizations [1]. They are published by agencies as diverse as the United States Department of Education, various state departments of education, and colleges and school districts in numerous parts of the country. Some of the research has come out of studies to determine the effectiveness of federal compensatory education programs.

These studies differ from each other in organization and vocabulary, but there are certain areas of agreement and they have a common educational thrust.

The indicators of effectiveness in this and in the following chapter are organized as a checklist that appears in Appendix A. Elements of effective schools that appear in nearly all of the studies are preceded by an asterisk in the checklist. These asterisked qualities are the ones you should look for in an effective school; they are presented here in more detail.

Clear School Mission or Purpose

The effective school has written statements describing its fundamental goals. These goals should enumerate the academic expectations for students. Staff, students, and parents need to be aware of what it is that the school seeks to accomplish, what students are expected to learn, and what the role of adults is in the learning process. Progress toward these goals is continually monitored because that which is measured tends to be accomplished.

Strong Administrative Leadership

Leadership is a critical factor in school effectiveness. The most important aspects of leadership are knowing what educational goals need to be accomplished and knowing how to utilize the available resources to move in that direction. Effective leadership presupposes a knowledge of curriculum. Curriculum means, simply, the organization of that which is to be learned. An effective leader continually monitors

Figure 6-1. The effective school leader stays close to the classroom and the instructional process.

classrooms and the teaching process (Figure 6-1). She/he will know what is going on in the educational process.

The principal or headmistress/master is the person responsible for seeing that the staff remains current in their knowledge of educational research and technology. Quality staff development or training is an ongoing outcome of good leadership. An effective staff, including teachers, principal and paraprofessionals, will continue to grow together. It is the building leader who is responsible for bringing the staff to a point where they can grow from each other's strengths and talents, and develop respect for one another.

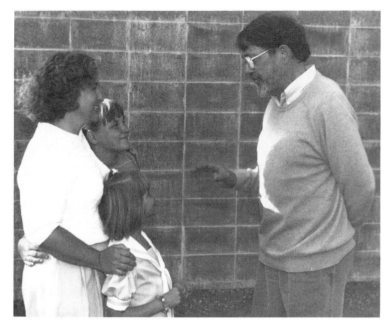

Figure 6-2. The effective leader is accessible to the staff, as well as to parents and students.

Further, the building leader must be accessible to staff, students, and parents (Figure 6-2) because hundreds of decisions affecting them are made in a school each day. The principal should assist in the decision-making process and be available to deal with problems before they reach crisis proportions.

Emphasis on Academic Achievement

The focus of the school should be academic so that the emphasis is on student learning and achievement in the basic skill areas. These are the subject areas, which, if learned well, will facilitate future learning and success on the job. Most important among these subjects are reading, written and oral language skills, and mathematics. Look for an indication that these academic goals and quality work are being accomplished and are recognized with incentives and rewards throughout the school. A focus on standards for each grade facilitates the accomplishment of goals for students.

In order to maintain maximum academic achievement, the body of educational research, indicating that there are certain more effective teaching strategies, must be put into practice. An understanding of child growth and development, knowledge of the psychology of learning and the appropriate sequence for introducing areas of instruction are all required for maximum learning to occur. The school must be viewed as a place not where *teaching* takes place, but where *learning* takes place. Measure the instructional practices against the information summarized in "What We Know About Learning" (Chapter 5).

Good work is a desired product of academic achievement. Student work needs to be displayed both in the classroom and throughout the school. Evidence of student work throughout the school makes a statement that both the work and the student are important and that students are making progress. Student work keeps the focus of the school on successful learning. Learning needs to be celebrated.

Homework is an extension of the educational program and is evident in quality schools. The assumption that each child has a quiet and suitable place at home to work is no longer accurate. The school needs to assist in making provisions for students to do work outside of the classroom.

Quality Instructional Staff

Education is a "people business," as reflected in the high percentage of the budget devoted to staff salaries. Therefore, the quality of the staff is critical to quality instruction (Figure 6-3). Several elements identify a good staff.

Variety

Variety on a staff is a strength. A staff that is all alike is ineffective and as unstimulating as a student body that is all alike. Variety in a staff, if properly utilized, is an agent for growth, as people who are different tend to stimulate each other. Older members have experience, while younger ones may have new techniques and enthusiasm. The interaction of the two is healthy and results in growth. Likewise, having staff members from various ethnic or cultural groups tends to help teachers develop the understanding that is necessary to deal effectively with students who are different. "Education is an exchange among people who are different!" [2]

Changing Staff

Movement of staff among schools can also be important. Lack of movement can lead to a certain amount of stagnation, and too much movement can undermine the continuity of ongoing educational programs and routines. Too much turnover on a staff can be an indicator of internal problems, such as dissension, unhappiness with school leadership, financial problems, or conflict with the central administration. What you are looking for is movement, not

Figure 6-3. The high quality of a teaching staff is critical to an effective school.

of people, but of ideas among people because this type of interchange will produce growth.

Continuing Education

No matter how good or how well educated a school staff is, educational methodologies change, research is accumulated, and schools change. The staff must change and grow to meet this need. In-service education must respond to the needs of the staff to keep them abreast of that which is current. Ongoing education is not only for teachers, but must include all staff, particularly the principal and paraprofessionals (Figure 6-3).

Volunteers

If all students could learn the same information the same way and in the same length of time, education would be simplified. However, since students need individual attention, the use of other individuals is critical to the educational process. Effective use of volunteers is one way to give attention to individual students, or to free the teacher from routines so that she/he may do so. Parents and community volunteers are considered part of the school staff. The school needs to organize so that volunteers can be wisely utilized.

Paraprofessionals

The first person a parent, and in many cases, a child, will meet is the school secretary. Since the attitude of parents and students toward a school is important, then those who create that attitude have to be attuned to their role in public relations. Both on the phone and in person, office personnel need to do their job effectively and leave a good impression. Do not ever underestimate the importance of the school secretary (Figure 6-4). This person is in a pivotal position in an effective organization and is a key element in determining a positive school climate.

Variety of Instructional Strategies

A variety of instructional strategies must be utilized to meet the needs of a broad range of individual differences.

Figure 6-4. The school secretary is a key person in an effective school.

Because schools serve a society of increasing diversity, the range of student abilities in classrooms is greater than ever before. Teachers need to utilize whole group, small group, and individual instruction. Various teaching skills need to meet the needs of students at various levels of growth. Technology, including the use of tape recorders, video tape, overhead projectors, calculators, and computers, help a good teacher be more effective in accommodating the learning styles of students.

School-wide programs must meet the needs of special needs students: slow learners, educationally handicapped, limited language proficient, and gifted.

High Expectations

The objectives in each subject area need to be defined and understood by teachers, students, and parents. There is a sequential development of skills that is articulated from one grade to another, and this information should be disseminated to the school community. Expectations should be high and aim at increasing student performance. A high success rate should be maintained in all areas of the curriculum. In addition to expected performance in school, homework expectations should be communicated to students and parents.

The quality of the instructional program is also important. Instruction needs to be structured so that it does not require only "yes/no" or "true/false" answers. Unfortunately, there has been too much emphasis on getting the "right answer" in the past. This has resulted in students who assume there is only one way to respond, solve a problem, and get an answer. Answers to most questions demand discussion. Higher-level thinking skills and techniques of creative problem solving are necessary in a changing technological world that demands a response from democratic citizens. Evidence should indicate that quality work is being accomplished and recognized with incentives and rewards throughout the school (Figure 6-5).

Safe and Orderly Environment

Good discipline cannot be overemphasized. For years, parents have indicated in public opinion polls that "school discipline" was the greatest problem facing education in this country. Maximum learning takes place in a school environment in which relationships among people are based on mutual respect, trust, and caring. Rules are established and communicated to students, staff, and parents. There is a clear statement of behavioral expectations. Consequences for poor behavior are fair and consistent. Good behavior is emphasized and recognized throughout the school. It is clear that all adults in the school are responsible for the behavior of all students.

Protection of Instructional Time

Nearly all recent studies of effective schools indicate that the more time spent on instruction, the more learning takes place. As a result, there has been widespread lengthing of both the school day and the school year. But increasing the time that students spend in school is not the only solution. The effective use of instructional time is probably more important. This is often referred to as "time on task." Techniques for wise utilization of instructional time include allocation of time reserved for basic subject areas; maintaining instructional time by reducing classroom interruptions;

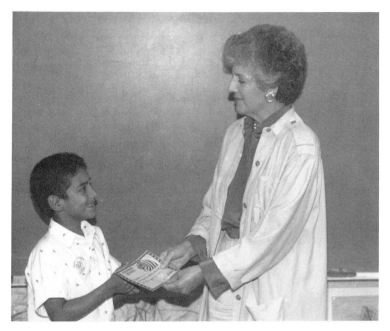

Figure 6-5. Good behavior is emphasized and recognized throughout the effective school.

reduction of absence and tardiness; reduction of time required to change rooms, subjects, or activities; and reduction of classroom bookkeeping trivia. There should be evidence that learning time is valued and protected. Very simply, the more time students spend on instructional tasks, the more they will learn.

Monitoring and Recognizing Student Progress

There must be an ongoing assessment program that focuses on the outcomes of student learning. This includes textbook and teacher-designed tests, which are used as regular recording procedures, and norm-referenced tests, which assess progress compared to other groups—district, diocese, state, and national. The testing program should be used to evaluate the instructional program, develop school goals, determine individual student progress, and plan for staff in-service activities. The major emphasis of assessment is to give students feedback regarding their educational progress. Look for evidence that the school participates in a standardized testing program, that the data is available, and that it is used for making educational decisions.

Positive Home–School Relationships

Effective schools are characterized by a strong degree of support from parents. Parents should be well-informed about the school program, disciplinary procedures, homework expectations, and their role in the educational process. In turn, they should support the school. Parental input and assistance is invited in a variety of ways (Figure 6-6). Parents should be evident at school, volunteering in classrooms, learning about the educational program, and providing input to the governance of the school.

Pupil progress should be reported in a timely and meaningful way to parents, and parents should have an opportunity to provide input to the teacher regarding the education of their child. In addition to regular reporting of individual progress of students, progress toward achieving the school's goals should also be reported to parents through newsletters from the principal, headmistress or headmaster, the PTA or parent group, and the classroom teachers.

Parents who are new to the school should have an opportunity to learn what the school is all about. Each school

Figure 6-6. An effective school is characterized by informed and supportive parents who contribute to the school in a variety of ways.

has unique qualities about which parents should be informed. Orientation for new parents, information about new or special programs, and discipline procedures should be available to parents in written form as well as through opportunities for visitation.

In addition to fulfilling its primary function—educating students—the school should be the center of other community activities. Other groups need to buy into the school. Organizations such as youth groups, groups promoting recreational activities, sports leagues, and adult groups should use the school facilities for a meeting place so that the school is viewed as the center of community activities.

Positive School Climate

Students need to experience positive feelings about their school and learning (Figure 6-7). School morale is reflected in the attitude of the students. Students who show pride and spirit in their school tend to be more involved academically. If they like school, they like learning. They should feel that their school is "the best," and there should be a strong and caring interaction between students and the adults in the school. This quality of caring is often referred to as "school climate." It can be observed but is very oftened

Figure 6-7. School climate is an attitude that will show in the interaction of students, staff, and parents. It can be seen in the faces of children and felt in the school.

determined more at a feeling level. "A positive school climate is both a means and an end. A good climate makes it possible to work productively toward important goals, such as academic learning, social development, and curriculum improvement." [3]

Student Involvement in the School

It is important for students, particularly as they get older, to feel that they have some "say" in their educational institution. There are various ways of placing value on student opinion. Student councils or some form of student representation in decision-making is one way. Another way is to actually monitor or solicit student opinion in a systematic way and to use this data in the decision-making process. The effect is the same. Students feel that how they feel is important and thus maintain an active interest in the operation of the school.

Self-Esteem of Students and Staff

Since learning takes place more effectively as a result of positive reinforcement rather than negative consequences, classrooms need to be organized to accentuate the positive activities that take place. A positive classroom also implies a high rate of success in learning. For maximum learning to take place, the success rate must be 75% and very often as high as 90% for all students in all activities. This kind of success rate demands a positive response and results in the growth of student self-esteem. Self-esteem is one of the most important factors to school success.

The staff, likewise, needs to have positive feelings about their mission. A positive mental attitude is critical for

Figure 6-8. The epitome of good intergroup relations is reached when differences are not only accepted but are valued by others.

educators because an educator's attitude is contagious and will affect others. In order for teachers to help students feel good about themselves, teachers have to feel good about themselves.

Good Intergroup Relations

Most schools are composed of various subgroups. These groups may be divided along ethnic, racial, or economic lines. It is important that the groups and individuals who are different from each other coexist in a positive way. The epitome of good intergroup relations is reached when differences are not only accepted but are valued by others (Figure 6-8).

Responsibility

It is also important that young children learn responsibility for use in future school experiences, to be independent on the job, and to be active members of a democratic society that presupposes responsible citizens. Beginning in kindergarten, students need the experience of getting milk, cleaning the chalkboards, and being messenger. In higher grades, older students should be entrusted with safety patrol, cross-age tutoring, moving classroom furniture, beating the erasers, and welcoming visitors to school. Students learn responsibility by taking responsibility.

References

1. A host of research on effective schools includes the following:

Brookover, W. and others. *Schools Can Make a Differ-*

ence. East Lansing, MI: Michigan State University, 1977.

California School Effectiveness Study. Sacramento, CA: California State Department of Education, 1977.

Denham, C. and Lieberman, A., Editors. *Time to Learn: A Review of the Beginning Teacher Evaluation Study.* Washington, DC: U.S. Government Printing Office, 1980.

Edmonds, R. and others. *Search for Effective Schools: The Identification and Analysis of City Schools That Are Instructionally Effective for Poor Children.* A Proposal for the National Institute of Education. Cambridge, MA: Harvard School for Education, 1977.

Elementary School, Evaluative Criteria. Falls Church, VA: National Study of School Evaluation, 1981.

Goodlad, J. *A Place Called School.* New York, NY: McGraw Hill, 1983.

Lake, S. "Characteristics of Effective Schools." San Mateo County Office of Education, undated.

Purkey, S. and Smith, M. "Effective Schools—A Review," *Elementary School Journal,* March 1983.

Rutter, M., et al. *Fifteen Thousand Hours.* Cambridge, MA: Harvard University Press, 1979.

"School Improvement Project: The Case Study Phase." New York: New York City Public Schools, 1979.

Venezky, R. and Winfield, L. "Schools That Succeed Beyond Expectations in Teaching Reading," University of Delaware Studies on Education, Newark, DE, August 9, 1979.

Westbrook, J. "Considering the Research: What Makes An Effective School?" Southwest Educational Development Laboratory, Austin, TX, September 1982.

Wilson, B. and Corcoran, T. "Places Where Children Succeed: A Profile of Outstanding Elementary Schools," Washington, DC: U.S. Government Printing Office, 1987.

"Why Do Some Urban Schools Succeed?" The Phi Delta Kappa Study of Exceptional Urban Elementary Schools. Bloomington, IN: Phi Delta Kappa, 1980.

2. Beery, K., Brokes, A., and Howlett, H. *The Guts To Grow.* Sioux Falls, SD: Dimensions Publishing, 1974, pp. v.

3. Fox, R., and all. *School Climate Improvement: A Challenge To The School Administrator.* Bloomington, IN: Phi Delta Kappa.

CHAPTER 7

Additional Important Considerations

Listed in the previous chapter are some of the most important characteristics of a good school that a parent may want to consider. There are many other elements that affect your choice of a school. Some have to do with the quality of the educational program. Some have to do with your personal preference. Some may be very subtle. Others may be very important to you and your child's education but not so important for another child. The factors contained in this chapter will also help you complete your rating of a school. These factors correlate to the checklist on pages 151-154.

Test Results

Standardized test results are probably the most misused measure of effective schools [1], yet they are probably the most common criteria that parents and, often, educators use to judge the quality of a particular school. Test results are something that parents can at least assume they understand. What could be easier than comparing the reading score in School A of 240 with the reading score in School B or 275 and saying that School B is the better school? What needs to be taken into account is that test results are not comparable as a measure of school quality unless the variables between the groups that are measured are comparable.

A number of factors can account for differences in test scores, specifically the higher score in School B. First, students in School B may know how to take tests better. Second, some of the students of lesser ability in School B may have been absent when the test was given. Third, there may be a number of limited-English-speaking students in School A who took the test without being able to read it. Fourth, testing conditions in School B may have been better than in School A (i.e., tested on a Friday before a holiday). Fifth, teachers in School A may have viewed the test as an intrusion into instructional time and not devoted adequate time to preparing for the test. Sixth, we may be comparing two schools with vastly different socioeconomic factors, making comparison unrealistic. Seventh, School B may have cheated on the test so that their results would look better. Eighth, School A may have a number of recently arrived, transient students who may test low.

Are these factors farfetched? Absolutely not! I have personally known them all to have occurred. So be careful about comparing schools on the basis of test results unless you have been trained in the interpretation of standardized test data.

Standardized test results do, however, serve very useful purposes. They are useful to measure growth and change in individual students and to show how they compare with other children in that grade. They show something about relative rank of groups of students, or indicate how a school compares with a standardized group. They give an indication of the effectiveness of a particular program if variables are known, thus providing baseline data for program evaluation. They compare like groups of students.

Also remember that the score you see is an *average* of all of the students who took that test. There may not be a single child who scored at the average. (See Figure 7-1.) You need to know how students who are similar to your child did. If you child is very bright, your question, in relation to test results, might be, "How well did the top 25% of children in that grade do in math?" You might find that the brighter students in School A did better than in School B.

Test scores do not give a full picture of a school. There are many variables to consider in evaluating schools and standardized test results by themselves are not a good measure to use in judging the quality of one school against another. They are, therefore, left out as a consideration on your check sheet in Appendix B. They do form a good basis for asking questions [2].

Financial Support

Adequate financial support is required to run a good school. In a private school, parents are an integral part of that financial support. In a public school, the institution is supported on the local, state, and federal level. Inquire

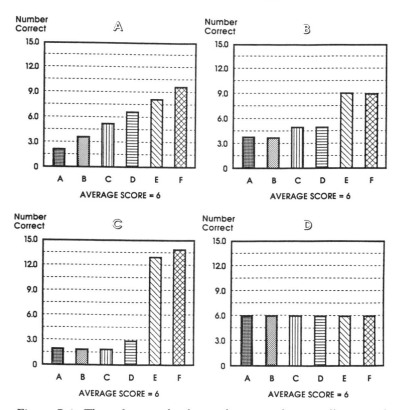

Figure 7-1. These four graphs depict the scores for a small group of students. Although 6 is the average score for all groups, it is a poor description for all except group D.

into the financial status of the district, particularly at the local level.

The most important ingredient in schools is good teachers. Their salaries are also the largest part of the financial budget. The books, learning materials, supplies, and equipment are important because they facilitate learning and enable the good teacher to make maximum use of teaching skills. Having the proper equipment means that the teacher uses energy to teach, not to procure the tools of learning. The use of modern technology enables educators to make maximum use of our knowledge of learning. Devices such as the overhead projector, videotape recorder, tape recorder, and computer perform a variety of functions that facilitate good teaching.

As stated, the most expensive item in a school budget is teacher salaries. The easiest way to "save money" is to increase class size so that fewer teachers are required. There is no magical formula for ideal class size. Smaller class size obviously allows more individual attention. In a school with a diverse population, this factor takes on considerable importance because of the need to individualize instruction and utilize a variety of teaching strategies. For certain activities, such as teaching written work, large class size is a distinct detriment. In considering schools, class size is a relative factor.

All teachers cannot be expert in all areas of the curriculum. Special teachers in certain areas of the curriculum can be more expert. These areas include physical education, music, art, library science, gifted, languages, and special education. Look for adequate personnel to teach the specialized subjects.

Physical Plant

An adequate physical plant provides the space to carry on the educational programs that operate within the school. Everyone enjoys modern, up-to-date facilities but they don't determine the quality of the school. The most important consideration is that the facilities enable learning to take place. To serve that purpose, they must be large enough, light enough, safe enough, and able to handle outside distractions adequately for teaching to proceed. Special areas need to adequately provide space for special programs.

Playground Area and Equipment

The school grounds are areas where students spend time before school, during recess and lunch, and often after school. The playground should provide the area to allow students to shift gears from classroom learning and to come in ready to resume the learning process. To that end, playgrounds with well-maintained equipment and grounds are important (Figure 7-2).

Assembly Area

An assembly area is important because it enables the student body to come together, receive information, participate in assemblies, and develop a sense of togetherness or school spirit. It is difficult to do this without some place to get students from various grade levels together. Therefore, a general assembly area is a consideration.

Accessible Library Facilities

In order for library books to be read, students need to be able to have access to the place where they are kept (Figure 7-3). Large collections are great, but what is more important is a library schedule that allows students to use the library. A circulation rate of at least three books per month per student would indicate effective use of a library.

Figure 7-2. Playgrounds are places that augment the growth that takes place in the classroom by giving children the opportunity to develop balance, coordination, large muscle control, and social interaction skills.

Statement of Policies

There are certain policies and procedures that should be clearly understood by parents (Figure 7-4). In most cases, these policies are in writing, while others are the school's typical modus operandi and could be clearly stated.

Statement of School Mission or Goals

The statement of the school mission or goals tells where the school is headed and what is being emphasized. In order to get everyone to buy in, it needs to be in writing.

Statement of Grade Level Expectations

There is a certain body of learning that is expected from each student at each grade level. These expectations need to be put in writing so that parents can understand what is being taught and assist in their accomplishment.

Curriculum by Subjects

Each school in a district develops a design for teaching subjects. It delineates the scope and sequence for that subject matter area. The purpose is to ensure that each teacher presents to students that information and those learnings

Figure 7-3. Accessibility of the library is a critical consideration.

Figure 7-4. School policies govern how the school is run. They need to be accessible and understood by children and parents.

that are deemed to be important by the governing body of the school or district. There should be a curriculum guide for each subject matter area. These documents are not static but should be under constant revision.

Student Behavior

Some document needs to detail the behavior policy of the school. It should be understood by students, parents, and teachers. It guarantees that students know what to expect and are treated equitably. It is this policy that guarantees that students will enjoy a safe, orderly learning environment.

Homework Policy

The homework policy should be clearly defined and communicated to teachers, students, and parents. It should explain that the amount of homework increases as the student progresses through the grades. In general, it should define expectations for daily homework, as well as for projects and long-term assignments.

Retention/Promotion Policy

There must be some basis on which the decision is made to promote or hold back a student to repeat a grade. This policy needs to take into account those factors that are considered in moving students from one grade to another. If a student is retained, what are the criteria on which this retention is based? If a student is promoted, on what basis is this decision made? These policies, which affect students so intimately, need to be available to parents [3].

Pupil Placement Policy

Students are assigned to a new teacher each year. There must be some rational basis for this assignment, which is reflected in the philosophy of the school. Students are grouped according to ability, assigned in order to maintain balance in classrooms, or just assigned by chance. If parent input is invited in placing a child, that needs to be stated.

Other Factors to Consider

After School Programs

Are there programs after school that your child might enjoy? You may want to explore youth groups, sports activities, music, arts and crafts, or extended day programs. These may be organized by the school or by outside agencies.

Child Care

If your child does not come directly home after school and needs child care, you should consider the school in relation to after-school child care programs. If these programs are not located on the school campus, is transportation available?

Ethnic Balance

Ethnic balance is not an element that is recognized by all parents as being important to their child's education. However, because America has a broad spectrum of racial and ethnic groups, the opportunity for children to grow up in a multicultural society is important. One of the greatest lessons a child can learn is to "judge people by the content of their character rather than by the color of their skin." [4] Whether or not the school achieves a good balance is a factor that must be judged by the individual parent.

Future of the School

Will the school that you choose still be available to your child next year? School enrollments are not static and this may necessitate changing attendance areas, changing grade levels that a school serves, or changing the magnet program within the school. It behooves the parent to inquire what projections have been made about the future of the school.

If you are considering a private school, what is planned in the future? Is the school expanding, shrinking, static? Why? In what way is the future of the school connected to finances?

Location

Where the school is located in relation to where you live can be an important consideration in choosing a school, especially if you have very small children. You may also want to look at the school neighborhood.

Magnet Programs

Remember, a magnet program is a curriculum designed to draw students from other schools because of its exemplary nature. A particular magnet program may be a very important consideration for you. It could be the major reason you want your child in a particular school. If so, you may wish to give it a weight of "2" or more on the checklist.

Reputation

A school's good reputation can be an advantage to students, especially if they have to compete to be admitted to the next school or college. There are certain schools, both public and private, that enjoy top-notch reputations for preparing students well. Bear in mind that reputation sometimes lag behind actual performance. Get information that is current and reliable from someone who would know—for instance, from an admittance office.

Transportation

If the school is not within walking distance, how do students get there? Is transportation provided? Is this a cost factor you need to consider?

Special Programs

If you have a child with a particular need, this could be a high priority in choosing a school. If your child has a physical handicap, a learning handicap, or has the need of an ESL program or other special program, this could be a primary consideration. You may want to give it particular emphasis on your rating sheet.

A private school may offer religious instruction. If it is sponsored by a church or religious group, there will probably be chapel. Determine what part of the curriculum is devoted to religious instruction and if that fits in with your own philosophy.

Personal Considerations

This is the section on your checklist where you should add your own considerations. They may play a part in your decision to choose one school over another. They may not be directly related to the quality of the educational program but need to be taken into account. You may, for instance, feel that developing creative ability in art is very important. List it as one of your criteria for comparison.

Financial considerations may play a part in your choice of schools. Is there a cost for books? Are uniforms required? Does the school require a time committment on your part? Are you expected to be part of yearly fundraising efforts? You may need to assign these factors a negative value. Anything that is important to you should be listed on your checklist and used as part of your rating scale.

References

1. "Dependence on Standardized Tests Puts Schools at Risk." *Issue Traces*, Burlingame, CA: Association of California School Administrators, Winter 1989.
2. *A Parent's Guide to Standardized Aptitude and Achievement Testing.* Arlington, VA: National School Public Relations Association, 1978.
3. Light, W. *A Parent Guide to Grade Retention.* Novato, CA: Academic Therapy Publications, 1981.
4. King, M. "I Have A Dream," from the speech delivered at the Poor Peoples' March in Washington, DC, August 28, 1963.

CHAPTER 8

The Effective
Teacher

The opportunity to select your child's teacher may present itself on occasion. However, parents will have fewer opportunities to select a teacher than they will in selecting a school. The reason is that classes are generally made up and assigned to a teacher in a purposeful way. That is, they are either balanced, with a mixture of students, or students may be homogeneously grouped for instruction, or certain children may be placed with a particular teacher because of learning styles or emotional factors. Allowing total parent choice of teachers would eliminate any plans the school has for instructional grouping. Furthermore, choosing teachers can turn into a popularity contest.

I think it is fair to say that an effective school is made up, for the most part, of effective teachers. If you are wise in the selection of a school, good teachers will be found there. The teacher is the most important factor in the educational process. The teacher is what makes the effective school happen. Recall your own school experience. There are very few people who can't remember a teacher who had a profound and lasting affect on their lives.

Identifying the Effective Teacher

An effective teacher might be defined as the person who brings about maximum social, emotional, and scholastic growth in students (Figure 8-1). Research has given us the tools to identify the effective school. Scientific identification of the effective teacher, however, has been much more elusive. Yet, the teacher is right at the heart of the educational program. What qualities do effective teachers possess?

A great many factors have been studied in an effort to identify good teachers [1] such as intelligence, knowledge of subject matter, educational background, professional education, cultural background, age, experience, sex, marital status, interests, voice and speech, and appearance. They have all been discounted as traits that might have any significant affect on good teaching [2]. It is interesting to observe that teachers exhibit wide diversity on these qualities.

The reason we have had such difficulty identifying the effective teacher is that we have focused on *what the teacher is* and what we should be looking at is *what the teacher does*. In other words, we need to evaluate what happens to students as rated against solid educational criteria. And where do we find solid educational criteria? We use the same factors that make an effective school and apply them to the classroom and find out if the teacher is making them happen with students. So remember, in order to find the good teacher, look at what is happening to students.

Figure 8-1. An effective teacher brings about maximum social, emotional, and scholastic growth in students.

With some modification, The "Effective Schools Checklist" on pages 151-154 can be used as an "Effective Teacher Checklist." In order to identify an effective teacher, compare the teacher with the items on the checklist that carry a weight of "2." Delete the items "Strong administrative leadership" and "Quality instructional staff." The remaining nine items, when thought of in terms of the classroom rather than the school in general, will give you a good rating scale for teachers. Certain personality factors are also considered.

Professional Qualities

Following are the factors that identify an effective school, interpreted to describe an effective teacher.

Has a clear mission or purpose. The teacher articulates the goals of school, as well as expectations in the classroom. Students know what is expected from them. Progress toward these goals is monitored regularly.

Emphasizes academic achievement. The teacher recognizes that the most important task of the elementary school is to maintain a strong program in basic skills. Expectations are maintained for each grade level. Student work is displayed, reflecting the emphasis on basic skills. Homework standards are articulated to students and parents.

Varies instructional strategies. The teacher uses a variety of student groupings to facilitate instruction. Recognition of various learning styles is reflected in the classroom organization. Technology is used to enhance the skills of the teacher. Programs are maintained for students with special needs.

Has high expectations. The effective teacher expects a lot and gets a lot. There is a high level of success evident in the classroom. Quality work is recognized.

A second aspect of a teacher's expectations is that the effective teacher accentuates the positive aspects of behavior. "Here's what to do," rather than "These are the things that you can't do."

Provides a safe and orderly environment. Behavioral expectations are made clear in the beginning of the year. Rules are uniformly enforced. Student, teacher, and parent roles are articulated. Good behavior is recognized. Emphasis is on student responsibility.

Protects instructional time. Maximum time is devoted to learning. The emphasis is on punctuality and regular attendance. Classroom interruptions are minimized.

Monitors student progress. The teacher uses the school-wide testing program in basic skills to measure progress of students against norms and to determine growth. Ongoing classroom testing evaluates learning and the effectiveness of teaching.

Encourages positive home–school relationships. The teacher strives for ongoing parent/teacher sharing and communication. Reporting pupil progress encourages the home and school to work in concert. Active parent involvement assists the teacher with a variety of classroom responsibilities.

Contributes to a positive school climate. High student morale is a goal that is aided by the teacher. Students should like school. Along with liking school, students realize that the educational process, both teaching and learning, is fun. Positive intergroup relations reflect teaching to appreciate individual differences.

Personal Qualities

Add to this scale four additional items that describe the personality of the good teacher (Figure 8-2).

Figure 8-2. Certain personality traits are very important in the effective teacher.

Loves children. The teacher must not only love the educational process, but children of all kinds. They must be loved and accepted for what they are, when they are good and when they act badly. The teacher must also really enjoy working with children at a particular stage of development. Not every kindergarten teacher will enjoy teaching emerging adolescents. Nor is a high-school teacher likely to appreciate first graders. In many cases, the teacher fulfills the role of the most stable influence in the child's life. Love of children is a must.

Has a sense of humor. Teaching is tough, exhausting, trying, often discouraging work. A sense of humor is what protects both the mental health of the teacher and of the classroom full of children. It is what keeps the educational process from becoming mechanized and hardened. It guarantees that the classroom remains a democratic institution and that children retain their right to the pursuit of happiness.

Respects the dignity of the individual. Respect will be shown in consideration for individuality and guarantee that each child will develop in her/his own way, at the proper speed, and remain her/his own person. The good teacher appreciates the unique experiences that each child brings to school. Respect fosters the development of democratic ideals.

Has a philosophy of growth. Educators must understand child growth and development so that the child is able to grow socially, emotionally, and intellectually and, in passing through the normal stages of growth, develop to the maximum of each of their unique potentials. The good teacher understands and uses these stages in development to maximize learning. Likewise, a good teacher considers that growth is part of her/his own professional life, too.

These personality characteristics, together with your checklist, will give you a good measure of the effective teacher.

References

1. Denham, C. and Lieberman, A., Editors. *Time to Learn: A Review of the Beginning Teacher Evaluation Study.* Washington, DC: U.S. Government Printing Office, 1980.

2. "Who's A Good Teacher?" Burlingame, CA: Joint Committee on Personnel Procedures, California School Boards Association and the California Teachers Association, 1960. (A monograph.)

CHAPTER 9

How To Gather Information

By now, you should have a pretty good idea of the kind of information you are seeking to determine the quality of the school in question. Now you need to gather the data you will use to rate the school on your checklist. How do you do this in a systematic way? Turn to Appendix A, "Effective Schools Checklist," and use this as a guide in collecting information. Note that it corresponds with and is explained in Chapters 6 and 7.

There are good sources of information and poor ones. Good sources include written information produced by the school or district, direct interviews with the principal or staff members, classroom visitations and observation, and interviews with current parents or students. Poor sources include real estate salespersons (their job is to sell houses, not understand educational programs), information from uninvolved adults in the community, most local newspapers (positive news does not sell as well as negative or sensational news), and people who attended the school some years ago. (The reputation of a school tends to lag about ten years behind actual practice.)

Written Information

Start with written information that is provided by the school district or governing body (Figure 9-1). Keep in mind that written material, such as brochures and informational handouts, will have certain qualities in common. They are produced to provide information for parents, but they are designed to create a good impression. They will, naturally, overlook any weaknesses. The emphasis here is to put the best foot forward. The major advantage for you is that it brings together information in one place without any effort on your part.

These documents should reveal certain trends of emphasis in the school district and provide you with a description of programs and services. Test results, names and locations of schools, and available demographic data will probably be discussed. They should also tell you something about the staff and about the in-service training activities. Additionally, they should describe the pupil progress reporting system and discuss the class size. Somewhere, there should be information about volunteers in the schools.

In general, these documents give an overall "feeling" or emphasis of what the district or school is like and in what direction it is headed. Those programs that are considered important by the district will be discussed in some detail. If you are in a district that encourages parent choice, has open enrollment, or has magnet schools, adequate information describing the various schools and programs should be

Figure 9-1. Both private and public schools will provide written information to parents describing their educational programs.

available to you. There will probably be information designed to assist you in choosing a school. Private schools have extensive information available since they survive through recruiting.

Visiting the School

All of these sources, however, provide secondhand information. In order to gather firsthand information, you need to arrange a visit. Bear in mind that not all schools are used to parents "shopping" before entering their child. Private schools, of course, are adept at explaining their program to parents. As plans that allow parents to pick their school grow [1], schools and school principals will become much more public-relations conscious and will be eager to show you around.

Call the school and talk to the principal. Explain that you are considering sending your child to her/his school and would like to visit. Explain that you would like to know as much as possible and would like to observe classrooms at the convenience of the teachers. Specify that you want to see a normal day rather than a special program. Indicate the grade level at which you wish to observe, and specify that you would also like to observe in a grade other than the grade your child(ren) will enter so that your judgment is based on the observation of more than one teacher. If there is a particular subject you want to see, so indicate. Try to schedule yourself in a classroom so that you will see a lesson from beginning to end. Request any written information about the school policies or procedures (see Chapter 7). Obtain this prior to your visit and become familiar with it. Your visit will be more meaningful.

Be sensitive as to when you schedule your visit. Children can be volatile, especially in groups. Elementary school children get very excited about holidays and events. Halloween, Christmas, just before spring or summer vacation, or during special programs can create a less-than-normal day. Certain other events can change the school schedule. A rainy day, for instance, creates a change in routine for students. Wind or cold may create more hyperactivity among children. Try to stay away from these times.

Request a brief meeting with the principal after the visit . . . that's when you will have the most meaningful questions. Request a copy of the latest PTA or parent club newsletter and the most recent newsletter from the principal.

Some schools have "Parent Visiting Days," which can work to your advantage as long as the school is not trying to put on a show. What you want is the average or typical day (if there is such a thing in school!). You want to know what goes on in the classroom on a daily basis. Request a map or diagram, if it is available, and use it to help you locate some of the places listed on your checklist. If there is a daily schedule or bell schedule, get one so that you don't enter an activity as it is being dismissed.

In an elementary school, there will be recess(es) and lunch. In higher grades there will also be a lunch break. Don't miss it. Take this opportunity to look over the grounds, see what children do when they are not closely supervised, observe how they interact with each other, and see what the rules of the playground are. See how children handle independent situations when they have more responsibility for their own behavior.

When you come to school to visit, always check in at the office. You may have an opportunity to talk with the school secretary briefly. Have a question or two ahead of time for this person (who knows a great deal about what goes on in the school). This is a good time to inquire about a parent with whom you can talk. Get the name of the PTA president or another knowledgeable parent to whom you can ask questions. It can be very helpful to see the school through another parent's eyes. Notice what is going on in the office. If new students are checking in, observe how they are handled. See how other parents are treated. See what is displayed in the office, as it will give you a clue about what is important in the school. Notice how school employees deal with each other.

There may be an orientation prior to your observation or you may be shown directly to a classroom. The teacher should be aware of your visit prior to your arrival. Upon entering, make your presence known to the teacher and be seated in an available chair. Remember that you are there to watch and see what goes on. Write down any questions to ask the teacher or principal later as time permits. Be sensitive about interrupting the classroom routine. You won't see what the classroom is really like if the teacher spends time talking to you.

Hopefully, you will have been able to schedule your visit so that you can see a lesson begin and end and then see the teacher change to another activity. In an elementary school, a period in which reading is taught may vary from thirty minutes to an hour depending on the grade level. Lessons in other subjects may be as brief as twenty minutes. Middle- and high-school classes usually vary from forty to fifty-five minutes.

The Classroom

You may feel a little self-conscious because you will probably be the only visitor. Rest assured that classrooms are used to visitors. Children see them all the time. After noticing you enter, they won't pay much attention to you

Figure 9-2. Notice everything in the classroom that indicates what activities are conducted.

unless you give some kind of a clue that you are there to help out. Don't do this. Send a child with a question or who is seeking assistance to the teacher. Any distractions will interrupt the normal program. Your focus will turn to giving information and you are in the classroom to gather it.

Following are some of the things you will want to observe in the classroom:

Non-educational activities. An important aspect of your observation is noticing classroom organization, including changing subjects or activities and housekeeping duties. Since the amount of time that students spend actually en-

Figure 9-3. Bulletin boards should be instructional as well as offer an opportunity to display the work of students.

gaged in learning activities can vary as much as 30% from teacher to teacher or school to school [2], this is a critical factor. Here is where you will see how important time constraints are to the teacher. How much time are children not on task? Notice if the class or teacher are disturbed during the time you observe.

Bulletin boards and displays. Look for children's work. Notice what kind of work is displayed (Figure 9-2). Is there a balance between art and academic work? Do bulletin boards reflect the educational emphasis in the classroom? Are there displays on which children are working (Figure

9-3)? Are certain procedures, such as classroom rules, in evidence? Remember, this is the place where your child will spend between five and six hours per day. Is the room generally attractive and pleasant?

The instructional process. Notice the interaction both between the teacher and students and among students (Figure 9-4). Knowing that children learn in a variety of ways, notice instruction that is directed by the teacher and learning that takes place as a result of pupil interaction. Observe how children are grouped. Is large group instruction utilized? Are children regrouped according to their achievement level for some learning? Notice the different strategies that are used by the teacher. Does the teacher appeal to the visual, auditory, and kinesthetic modes of learning [3]? Notice the rate of success among students as they do independent work. Notice what children do when their assignment is finished and how smoothly they move into that activity. Do they seem to take responsibility for their own learning, once they understand what is expected?

Discipline. It is important to note how the disruptive student is handled. It is also important to notice if there isn't a disruptive student. Observe the positive reinforcement that is given by the teacher. Does she call attention to the positive behavior by saying that is what she likes? Does poor behavior take away from instructional time? Are there negative aspects to the discipline system? Do the rules seem to be clearly understood by everyone?

When you leave. there is not a teacher in the world who, when an observer leaves the classroom, wonders what that person thought! Give the teacher some feedback and keep

Figure 9-4. Notice the interaction between teacher and students and also among students.

it positive (Figure 9-5). Write the teacher a brief note calling attention to something that occurred during the time you were in the classroom that was done well or handled well. Without being judgmental, simply jot down a few lines. For instance you might say, "I enjoyed the discussion you led about the *Story of Stuart Little.* You certainly seem to make your students think. Thanks for letting me observe." A comment like this will make you welcome next time.

Now, if you haven't been taking notes, jot down some of your observations. You will be surprised how much you may forget if you are visiting several classrooms. Fill in those areas on the "Effective Schools Checklist" that are appropriate. On the basis of your classroom visitation, decide what questions you need to ask the principal or what information you still need.

Figure 9-5. Let the teacher know that you appreciated the opportunity to visit and observe in the classroom.

References

1. McCurdy, J. "Choices in Schools: What's Ahead and What to Do." *Education USA* (Special Report), Arlington, VA: National School Public Relations Association, 1985.
2. Denham, C. and Lieberman, A., Editors. *Time to Learn: A Review of the Beginning Teacher Evaluation Study.* Washington, DC: U.S. Government Printing Office, 1980.
3. Riessman, F. "Styles of Learning." *NEA Journal,* March 1966.

CHAPTER 10

The Parent's Role

As a parent, you are vitally interested in your child's education. You have taken the time to learn how to determine the effectiveness of a school. You know how to recognize good teaching. You know what to look for in an educational institution. Now, let's consider one of the most important elements in determining the success of your child's scholastic endeavors: You, the child's parent.

The evaluation of education must take into account what I call "The Triangle of Learning," which contains three elements (Figure 10-1). You, the parent, form the first corner. You have brought the child into being. You became the child's first teacher and provided the preparation for formal learning. The child's early success in school is dependent upon you. You have created the attitudes and habits that will affect the child's ability to take advantage of an education. You will continue the support that is needed for the child to make normal progress.

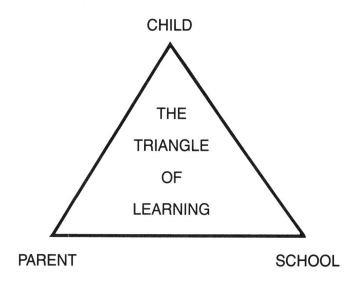

CHILD

THE

TRIANGLE

OF

LEARNING

PARENT   SCHOOL

Figure 10-1. The triangle of learning.

The child is the object of the educational effort and forms the second corner of the triangle. Her/his personality, attitudes, and motivation will be more important than the child's native ability. How successful a student feels she/he can be will determine, to a large extent, the degree of success which will be achieved. Here, too, the parent plays an important role in fostering the child's self-esteem and belief in her/his ability to achieve success.

The school, its leadership, teachers, facilities, and organization are the third corner. They provide the setting in which the child will be educationally nurtured and learning will take place. A good school and good teachers will con-

Figure 10-2. The learning triangle includes the child, the parent, and the teacher.

tinue the educational process which has been begun by the parents.

Don't evaluate your child's educational institution without taking all three elements into account, for the learning triangle will not exist without any one (Figure 10-2).

What You Can Do

Since you, as a parent, are so important, let's take a look at some of the things you can do to improve your child's chance of success in school (Figure 10-3). Some will seem so obvious that you don't think they need to be stated. You would be surprised how many parents overlook a child's basic needs and expect the school to educate her/him.

Take Care of Your Child's Physical Needs

A prerequisite for entering school is a physical exam. Be sure that medical problems do not interfere with your child's ability to learn. Have problems diagnosed and treated. You would be surprised to know how many children have been considered of below normal intelligence or as having a learning handicap, only to learn that a physical problem, such

Figure 10-3. Nothing has as great an effect on learning as the attitude and preparation that is begun in the home.

as a visual or hearing deficit, interfered with learning. When your child comes to school, make sure that she/he is adequately dressed, bathed, and fed. If a child's attention turns to needs of a physical nature, attention cannot be focused on mental tasks. Adequate sleep and nutrition are essential for a student's brain to operate efficiently. Send your child to school rested and with something nutritional for breakfast.

Provide for Your Child's Emotional Needs

A child needs to come to school with a mental set that allows the mind to function without being encumbered. Although only a minority of children suffer from such serious emotional traumas as molestation or physical abuse, many more will be emotionally deprived as a result of domestic discord, divorce, custody battles, or economic worries. Don't get into a heated discussion with your child before school. For your child, the tone of the day at school is often determined by how she/he starts the day at home. A child must feel loved and secure to learn well.

Engage Your Child in Conversation

A child first learns to talk by hearing you talk. Basic vocabulary skills are learned early and easily. Besides talking to your child, you must also listen so that speaking skills can be practiced and improved. The more a child talks, the better she/he is likely to read [1]. Talking is also impor-tant for family problem solving. The home should provide an environment in which the child feels comfortable to discuss openly any problem that he/she may have and suggest solutions. Show her/him that you are interested in the daily occurrences at school. Discuss the happenings at school. Don't accept the answer, "Nothing" to the question, "What did you do in school today?" That is not an adequate description of six hours at school.

Show Interest in Your Child

Whatever occupies your child's mind is important. You need to show that it is also important to you. School is your child's life and it is as important as your job is to you. Parents need to ask if there is any homework and see that it is completed, giving help when needed. Work brought home by the child needs its own place of importance. Show that you are proud of what has been accomplished. Give praise and build on the success your child achieves. Your child's self-confidence is critical to success in school.

Consider the Importance of Attendance

Get your child to school regularly and one time. A child is bound to get upset if she/he arrives when the lunch report or attendance has just gone to the office, the teacher is in the middle of a reading group, the class has settled down with their morning's work, or has left on a field trip. Punctuality is a habit that is formed early. It is a primary requirement of most employers. Missing school creates gaps that are not always completely filled in. Being late for school has an adverse affect on the child because (1) the child misses instruction, (2) the child begins to form a habit, and (3) the child begins to draw resentment from other students for disturbing the class or having to go back and start over.

Emphasize Reading at Home

No skill is more important to school success than reading (Figure 10-4). Reading must be valued and practiced as part of family life. Children need to see parents read in order to develop the interest. "The best way for parents to help their children become better readers is to read to them— even when they are very young." [2] As your child becomes older, buy books to read that are at an appropriate level for your child. Ask your child's teacher or librarian for help in choosing books. As a family, use the library and read books, magazines, and newspapers at home. Turning off the television is essential. Give your child meaningful tasks that require reading signs, posters, labels in the market, shopping lists, etc. It is possible for a child to learn to read off a

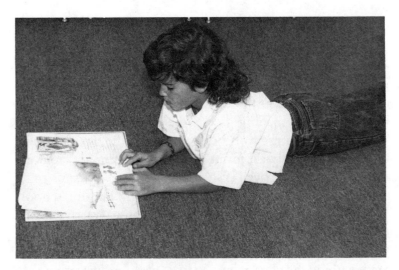

Figure 10-4. Parents who help their children value the habit of reading will have students who are successful readers.

cereal box! Some time ago, a survey showed that the most commonly recognized word by children in America was "Coca Cola." That wasn't learned at school! If the child's language is other than English, read in that language and have the child read in that language. Regardless of the language, children only need to learn to read once.

Create the Habit of Writing

Expressing one's ideas in writing is such an important skill to success in life that it cannot be entirely left to the school. Help your child to put thoughts down on paper. "Even toddlers, who can hardly hold a crayon or pencil are eager to 'write' long before they acquire the skills in kindergarten that formally prepare them to read and write." [3] Encourage writing letters. Keeping a journal is an excellent activity, either on a trip or at home. Be helpful in improving the writing process by giving your child feedback. With the advent of the computer, a word processing program will help your child get her/his thoughts down on paper easily.

Use Mathematics in the Home

Provide opportunities for your child to use numbers in the home. Teach counting and one-to-one relationships [4]. The math you teach at home should be of a very practical nature (Figure 10-5). Encourage assistance in the kitchen, such as helping with cooking and baking with particular emphasis on measuring. Build things with your child that require measuring. Use weighing, and provide lots of practice with money and making change.

Figure 10-5. A good basis for mathematics is provided through practical experience in the home.

Encourage Good Study Habits

Studying is a habit that parents are instrumental in developing. The skill does not come easily; it needs to be developed. Good study habits pay off throughout the years. Establish a good, quiet place and provide all the tools that are required—books, dictionary, pencils, paper, etc. Decide on a regular time to study and provide an environment that allows thinking to take place by eliminating distractions and interruptions. Help your child use some study methods like skimming, taking an overview, keeping notes, organizing material, and knowing how to use resources.

Develop Responsibility

Children need to contribute to the family and feel that what they do in the home is important. A sense of pride needs to be instilled, knowing that what they do helps the family. Create a structured home environment so that a child knows what to expect. Chores in the home help the child develop a responsible attitude in school and in later life. Expect your child to take care of and respect his/her property and the property of others. Rules need to be established and when they are broken, fair and consistent consequences must follow. Praise and acceptance must follow positive behavior and adherence to family expectations.

Limit Television

The average American child will spend more time watching television than time in school [5]. I cannot say that there is nothing worth watching on television; however, television needs to be de-emphasized (Figure 10-6).

Television introduces children to social situations that they are not mature enough to handle. Television is permeated with violence. It casts many people in inappropriate roles—the heroes and villains. It simplifies problem solving and it can create frustration by depicting life situations most people cannot achieve. It helps children learn to tune out people in real life. It provides input without requiring any thought processing or output of ideas. It creates an expectation that teaching needs to be entertaining.

Figure 10-6. Control of the television is critical if parents are to have successful students.

All of these are negative aspects of television, but none quite as important as the fact that television is robbing children of a productive childhood. It takes time from such activities as reading, family conversation, organizing games and playing with other children, building or working on crafts, playing with animals, and all of the childhood activities that are productive because they require thought and action. "More time spent viewing means less time for more intellectual activities." [6]

Maintain a Positive Attitude Toward the School

Perhaps the most important factor of all is your interaction with the school. Your child will reflect your attitude toward school and learning. If education is important to you, it will be important to your child. Parental influence is a critical factor and this influence can either reinforce or negate school values and attitudes. Your getting involved in school gives the school value in the mind of the child. Your being active in school affairs keeps you informed long after you have chosen a school.

Rest assured that if you continue the interest you are showing in the education of your child, your child will achieve success in school.

References

1. WHAT WORKS: Research About Teaching and Learning. Washington, DC: United States Department of Education. 1987, pp. 12.
2. Ibid., pp. 7.
3. Ibid., pp. 9.
4. Ibid., pp. 11.
5. Winn, M. The Plug-In Drug. New York, NY: The Viking Press, 1978, pp. 4.
6. WHAT WORKS, op. cit., pp. 13.

CHAPTER 11

After You Choose Your Child's School

The preceding chapters explained the operation of schools today and how they have changed. An attempt has been made to help you look at your own child and evaluate her/his personality and needs, rather than your own, in order to determine the kind of school program that will be most beneficial. Information has been provided to help you understand the learning process, for if you understand learning, you have a much more valid basis for judging a good school.

Appendix B will help you understand the normal growth and development characteristics that typify children at various ages, and explain what you can expect to be taught to your children at different grade levels. You now have a checklist (pages 151-154) to help you evaluate a school against criteria which have been shown, by an extensive body of research, to be typical of the effective school. You have the criteria by which you can judge the good teacher.

Finally, you now know how to gather the data you need to help you make a school choice.

Once you have made your decision, how do you get your child into the school you have chosen? Public schools generally divide communities into geographical attendance areas. If you have moved into a particular attendance area, your child(ren) may be required to attend the school that serves that area. However, don't make that assumption without asking. That school may be full and your child could be bussed elsewhere.

Or, you may have a choice of schools. Make sure that you understand the options that are available to you. These may be available because of desegregation requirements, "parent choice" laws, magnet programs, child-care provisions in the law, the need for special programs such as special education or bilingual education, or general open enrollment policies. Options may be made available to you by the local school district or provisions in the state law. Be sure to inquire. If you are moving into an area so that your child can attend a particular school, you should obtain attendance information in advance.

For either public or private schools, find out what the application process is and when the application is due. Determine if certain records are required. Some schools will require that application is made the previous year, sometimes as early as January. Is there an interview process? Are testing or recommendations required? This is typical of some independent private schools. Do you need to provide the school with health records or previous transcripts?

If you have chosen a private school, there will be additional financial considerations. Find out when payments are due, whether or not scholarships are available, and if there is a reduction in cost if siblings are enrolled. Find out how and when the decision to admit your child is made.

If your request to attend a particular school is denied, this may not be the end. In public schools, there is always a chain of command. If you feel strongly, don't be afraid to appeal beyond the principal to the superintendent, the local school board, or the county board of education. You are making a decision affecting your child's future. If you are not an advocate for your child, who will be? Remember, you are making an investment of more than $60,000. Use the information that you have and make your decision wisely!

APPENDIX A

Effective
Schools Checklist

DIRECTIONS:

Below are 23 points to consider in judging a quality school. Additional space is given to add any personal considerations you may have. Under each main heading are some of the things to look for to determine a score for each item. The first eleven items are generally agreed to be critical in determining quality and are therefore weighted. All items are detailed in Chapters 7 and 8. Rate each item on the scale from 0 (None) to 3 (Good). Multiply the weighted items by two and record the score. Total a score in the space provided. This form may be duplicated for your personal use.

	Wt.	None	Poor	OK	Good	Score
1. Clear school mission or purpose • Goals of school are articulated • Student expectations defined • Progress monitored	(2)	—	—	—	—	☐
2. Strong administrative leadership • Knowledgeable of curriculum • Accessible to staff and students • Monitors classrooms and teaching • On-going staff development	(2)	—	—	—	—	☐

	Wt.	None	Poor	OK	Good	Score

3. Emphasis on academic (2) — — — — ☐
   achievement
   • Strong program in basic skills
   • Expectations by grade level
   • Valid teaching strategies
   • Display of students' work
   • Homework standards articulated

4. Quality instructional staff (2) — — — — ☐
   • Quality selection criteria
   • Variety of teacher types
   • Staff stability
   • On-going staff in-service
   • Use of volunteers
   • Quality secretary

5. Variety of instructional strategies (2) — — — — ☐
   • Student grouping for instruction
   • Recognition of various
     learning styles
   • Use of technology
   • Programs for special needs

6. High expectations (2) — — — — ☐
   • Communication of expectations
   • High level of success
   • Recognition of quality work

7. Safe and orderly environment (2) — — — — ☐
   • Clear behavioral expectations
   • Rules are uniformly enforced
   • Student, staff, parent roles
     articulated
   • Good behavior recognized

8. Protection of instructional time (2) — — — — ☐
   • Maximum time on task
   • Emphasis on punctuality/attendance
   • Classroom interruptions minimized
   • Instructional time protected

9. Monitoring of student progress (2) — — — — ☐
   • School-wide testing in basic skills
   • On-going classroom testing
   • Monitoring of student opinion

	Wt.	None	Poor	OK	Good	Score
10. Positive home–school relationships • Ongoing parent/teacher sharing • Reporting of pupil progress • Use of school volunteers • Active parent involvement • After-school programs—community use	(2)	—	—	—	—	☐
11. Positive school climate • High student morale • Positive intergroup relations • Emphasis on student responsibility • Cohesive school spirit	(2)	—	—	—	—	☐
12. Financial support • Textbooks, materials, technology • Class size • Special staff		—	—	—	—	☐
13. Physical plant • Classrooms • Playground area and equipment • Assembly area • Assessible library facilities		—	—	—	—	☐
14. Statement of policies • School mission • Grade level expectations • Curriculum by subjects • Student behavior • Homework • Retention/promotion • Pupil Placement • Absence/tardiness		—	—	—	—	☐
15. After School Programs		—	—	—	—	☐
16. Child Care		—	—	—	—	☐
17. Ethnic balance		—	—	—	—	☐
18. Future of the School		—	—	—	—	☐
19. Location		—	—	—	—	☐

	Wt.	None	Poor	OK	Good	Score
20. Magnet Program		—	—	—	—	☐
21. Reputation		—	—	—	—	☐
22. Special Programs		—	—	—	—	☐
23. Transportation		—	—	—	—	☐
24. Other Personal Considerations		—	—	—	—	☐
_____		—	—	—	—	☐
_____		—	—	—	—	☐
_____		—	—	—	—	☐

Name of School ————————————————

Total Score .... ————————

Comments:
_____
_____
_____
_____
_____

APPENDIX B

Growth and Learning Expectations

Appendix B provides an overview of (1) what children are like at various grade or age levels and (2) what is generally expected to be taught at each grade. The typical growth characteristics for children at each grade level are listed, followed by the typical curriculum. This gives parents a frame of reference with which to compare the child within the school setting.

You may want to find the section that deals with the grade level of your child and familiarize yourself with that. Perhaps the year before and the year after would help you to put the current year into perspective. You will find some characteristics carrying over or emerging early. As your child grows and changes, you may find that some of the behaviors you worried about are perfectly normal aspects of the growth pattern of children.

Growth Characteristics of School-age Children

Kindergarten Growth Characteristics

- Adjusts with relative ease to a school situation even though it is a new experience
- May want a parent to accompany her/him on the first day(s) of school
- May want to take a favorite toy or a book to share to school
- Seeks teacher recognition for doing a good job
- Doesn't usually communicate much about what happens in school
- Likes to go directly to her/his classroom when arriving at school
- Enjoys a routine that also allows freedom of movement
- Plays house and plays with blocks
- Enjoys directed activity periods of about twenty minutes
- Likes signs and may begin to recognize words and letters
- Becomes interested in numbers and enjoys counting
- Enjoys story time and stories which have repetitive action and phrases
- Works in short bursts of energy and attention span is not more than twenty minutes
- Likes to be in a group but plays on her/his own
- Accepts and likes the teacher and regards her/him as the authority
- May complain about "having to do things"
- Likes to talk but also likes to listen to stories
- Does not readily distinguish between reality and fantasy
- Likes to dress up in adult clothes

First-Grade Growth Characteristics

- Shows a positive anticipation for the start of school
- Likes school and wants to learn
- May refuse to go to school because of an unpleasant experience
- May still show some evidence of fatigue during a full-day program
- Brings many things from home to share
- Enjoys parent approval for work completed at school
- Doesn't report much on what happens at school
- Shows ups and downs and wide swings in behavior
- Likes to begin new activities
- Likes group oral work
- Begins to write using capital letters and shows some reversals
- Likes to be read to and begins to read groups of words
- Likes to explore illustrated books
- Begins to use number symbols
- Moves from one activity to another and can continue an activity the next day
- Begins to play in a group or with one or two friends
- Likes to conform to the teacher's demands and please her/him
- Feels the teacher's word is law
- May not know when to ask the teacher for help
- Needs teacher approval and acceptance
- Likes to talk and use big words
- Makes errors in reading/counting but learns from the mistakes

Second-Grade Growth Characteristics

- May feel that second grade will be too difficult
- Forms closer attachments to the teacher; boys may have crushes
- Likes to share things with class and teacher
- Doesn't want to be walked to school by mother
- Collects many things in her/his desk rather than taking home
- Tends to be more forgetful about school events/details
- Can be restless, active, talkative, and need movement or change of pace
- Manipulates objects, pencils, erasers, crayons, and other objects in the desk
- Very dependent and needs constant reinforcement from the teacher; wants to be right, may worry about approval
- May not be able to copy well from the chalkboard
- Reads sentences reasonably well, and oral reading begins to have fluency and feeling
- Likes to be involved in oral activities: Simon Says, oral arithmetic, etc.
- Plays with great enthusiasm; even gets "carried away"
- Becomes involved in group play and activities
- May act up when teacher is out of the classroom
- Begins to enjoy ball activities
- Sex differences become more apparent in activities; boys wanting to build, girls to play dolls
- Tends to perservere on a task and sometimes must be stopped
- Communicates well and uses sentence structure in conversation; shows more maturity
- Individual differences are more apparent; children show

readiness for school activities at different stages
- May make sounds with mouth and become noisy during the change of activities

Third-Grade Growth Characteristics

- Enjoys school and the events in school life
- May dawdle and have trouble being on time for school
- Not as dependent on the teacher; looks upon her/him as a friend or part of his group
- Begins to develop group or class loyalty
- More information about what goes on at school is told at home; takes home work and projects
- Brings things to school that have to do with school work
- Is concerned about what the group is doing, especially if having to miss school
- Is enthusiastic upon entering the classroom, participating in a discussion, answering questions
- Is able to copy from the chalkboard and work more independently without as much teacher interaction
- Becomes aware of her/his place in a group and knows who is "best" in different activities
- Is able to do independent reading and can handle interruption and return to work
- Is able to do cursive writing and can sometimes write a short story
- Can play an organized game for an entire recess period
- Likes to help the teacher and help out in the classroom
- Articulates feelings and experiences more like an adult
- Is more aware of what is going on around and may be distracted; may work better if separated from group

Fourth-Grade Growth Characteristics

- Is able to take responsibility for getting to school on time
- Likes to talk about home activities, television programs, movies
- Likes and becomes devoted to the teacher but likes to see her/him make a mistake
- Is comfortable with a schedule in the classroom and is aware of any deviation
- Has become more independent and doesn't want help from the teacher until she/he asks
- Has definite likes and dislikes in subjects and arithmetic comes into focus
- Very concerned about being treated fairly
- Develops much more individuality in appearance and behavior
- Likes to do well in school work and make good grades
- Is becoming aware of her/his own learning strengths and limitations
- Has developed enough self-discipline to carry through on an extended school project
- Is using reading as a means of obtaining information in many areas
- Is able to do handwriting in a more controlled, adult way, particularly girls
- Is forming individual friendships; boys and girls often separate when playing games or have free time
- Sex differences begin to become apparent and girls may mature more rapidly than boys
- Writing for communication is well-developed
- May become self-conscious speaking before a group
- Is becoming more competitive in work and on the playground

Fifth-Grade Growth Characteristics

- Generally likes school and likes to be taught
- Respects teacher and regards her/his word as law but is beginning to notice physical appearance
- Begins to like and identify with great heros
- Takes dictation well but handwriting may not be as precise as in third or fourth grade
- Likes to listen to stories and likes to read for extended periods
- Is able to memorize lengthy passages
- Is able to grasp material presented visually or orally
- Is beginning to like organized sports
- Likes music and likes to sing
- Feels secure with a schedule in school
- Enjoys learning facts
- Is accepting of the opposite sex and is beginning to become aware of sexual differences
- Begins to see social acceptance as important
- Begins passing notes and having secrets
- Enjoys oral arithmetic
- Responds to firmness but wants the teacher to be fair

Sixth-Grade Growth Characteristics

- Tends to like school but is becoming critical of school and the teacher
- Finds that social relationships and acceptance are becoming very important
- Wants a teacher who makes students work hard but who has a sense of humor
- Likes to be teased by the teacher on a friendly basis
- Tends to gather in groups separated on the basis of sex

- Is beginning to look to peers for leadership
- Is becoming much more restless, wriggly, and more explosive; has a shorter attention span
- Is interested in team sports; some girls are also becoming interested, not much patience or kindness with the poor player
- Is able to take on long-range assignments but may need reminding and scheduling
- Likes competition and classroom games
- Is good at memorizing facts but has trouble seeing relationships
- Likes good stories
- Tends to fatigue easily toward the end of school
- Becomes involved in nudging, poking, teasing, chasing
- Enjoys and needs non-academic school activities: shop, physical education, music, art, drama
- Tends to have strong feelings about arithmetic
- Needs some help in organizing homework so that it is not left to the last minute

Seventh-Grade Growth Characteristics

- Is often carried away by enthusiasm
- Drawn toward others and is very much group-oriented—girls particularly flock together and discuss social activities. Very much aware of personal appearance
- Is less dependent on the teacher than previously, tends to like the teacher but wants one who is firm, has a sense of humor, and, above all, knows how to teach
- In absence of teacher or with a weak teacher, can be a discipline problem; needs a firm hand
- Usually likes arithmetic
- Likes to debate and argue

- Is beginning to enjoy lighter adult literature, adventure, and books that stretch the imagination; boys' and girls' tastes differ
- Enjoys the non-academic subjects—shop, physical education, art, music, cooking, sewing, drama
- Very outspoken about opinions both in school and with parents
- Girls are very interested in boys
- Generally, can become restless in class over extended periods

Eighth-Grade Growth Characteristics

- Tends to be happier in school and is more ready to settle down to learning
- Needs a firm hand from the teacher or would join the group and get out of control
- Likes a teacher who is firm, fair, and understanding; a sense of humor helps
- Likes to carry on discussions of a fairly adult nature with the teacher
- Is better able to organize time, use self-control, and show responsibility
- Needs strong guidance
- Very concerned with social activities, parties, weekend activities
- Very much into physical education but does not necessarily like showering in public
- May begin to dislike the principal as an authority figure
- Boys and girls alike tend to become more prolific readers
- Those who are good in math may become very adept with computers

- Is beginning to recognize that social issues are not all black-or-white and is willing to search for more information
- Boys talk about girls and girls talk about older boys

Grade Level Expectancies

Following is a detailed breakdown of what is generally expected to be taught at each grade level. Although there is no such thing as a "national curriculum," there is general agreement regarding skills that should be taught at each grade level. Various states, school districts, and private schools will not vary a great deal regarding teaching certain skills at specific grade levels. Remember, these are guidelines and may vary somewhat from school to school.

Expectancies are listed in the areas of art, citizenship, health, homework, language, mathematics, music, physical education, reading, science, and social studies.

Kindergarten Expectancies

Art

- Learns to use scissors, paste, paint, crayons, paper, chalk
- Learns to express ideas through art
- Creates seasonal projects
- Learns to appreciate art objects

Citizenship

- Develops positive attitude toward authority
- Learns leadership/followership
- Learns about American heritage
- Demonstrates moral understandings
- Understands rights of others

Health

- Awareness of proper nutrition
- Awareness of proper dental care
- Awareness of role of exercise

Language

Listening/Speaking
- Follows oral directions
- Listens to stories
- Identifies familiar sounds
- Identifies named objects
- Identifies pictured objects
- Tells first and last name
- Recalls events in sequence
- Speaks in sentences
- Shares ideas in groups
- Names familiar objects
- Memorizes rhymes, poems, songs
- Participates in imaginative play
- Asks appropriate questions

Composition (Grammar/Usage/Writing)
- Dictates a complete story
- Completes open-ended sentences

Handwriting
- Uses pencil and paper correctly
- Copies letters and words
- Writes complete name
- Traces patterns on paper
- Writes from left to right

Study Skills
- Learns to work independently
- Learns to mark responses
- Identifies alphabet letters by name

Mathematics

Basic Computation
- Rote counts to 50
- Recognizes and writes numerals 1–20
- Matches objects to numerals 1–10
- Arranges objects in patterns

Measurement
- Names and assigns simple money value
- Compares length (longer–shorter)
- Compares greater than, less than, equal to
- Compares heavier–lighter
- Understands beginning time concepts

Geometry
- Identifies common geometric shapes
- Identifies simple fractional parts

Music

- Learns to enjoy music

- Learns holiday, folk, patriotic songs
- Begins understanding of rhythm

Physical Education

- Ball skills—throwing/catching
- Running, skipping, hopping, jumping
- Uses playground equipment
- Develops balance, coordination
- Begins recreational games
- Applies taking turns

Reading

Discrimination/Auditory
- Recognizes beginning sounds of words
- Recognizes ending sounds of words
- Recognizes letter-sound correspondence
- Recognizes same and different
- Recognizes rhyming words

Discrimination/Visual
- Recognizes upper- and lower-case letters
- Writes numerals
- Identifies colors
- Identifies shapes and sizes
- Duplicates patterns
- Matches pictures and words

Vocabulary
- Reads name
- Reads color words
- Reads number words
- Reads selected vocabulary

Comprehension
- Understands "likes" and "opposites"
- Understands main idea of stories
- Retells events in sequence
- Distinguishes fact and fiction
- Draws conclusions
- Categorizes objects

Literature
- Uses a book properly
- Listens to stories
- Learns correct use of library
- Develops a desire to share books

Science

The study of science differs from district to district but may include all or some of the following:

- Awareness of weather
- Awareness of seasons
- Difference between living/non-living things
- Relationships among living things
- Awareness of growth and development

Social Studies

- Understanding the role of food and shelter
- Role of the family
- Interaction with friends
- Understanding of cultural differences
- Special holidays and occasions
- Understanding the concept of sharing

First-Grade Expectancies

Art

- Develops eye/hand coordination
- Creates seasonal projects
- Develops expression through art
- Works with a variety of media

Citizenship

- Develops positive attitude toward authority
- Learns leadership/followership
- Develops appreciation of American heritage
- Develops moral understandings
- Understands rights of others

Health

- Dental health
- Nutrition, diet, rest
- Basic home/school safety practices

Language

Listening/Speaking
- Follows oral directions
- Recalls events in sequence
- Participates in discussion
- Memorizes songs/poems
- Repeats verbatim a 12–15 syllable sentence
- Tells birthday
- Tells full address

- Listens to recall details
- Understands positional vocabulary

Composition (Grammar/Usage/Writing)

- Dictates complete sentence
- Dictates complete story
- Writes complete sentence
- Completes open-ended sentence
- Capitalizes first letter of names
- Capitalizes first word in sentence
- Capitalizes the word "I"
- Uses period at end of sentence
- Forms alphabet letters correctly
- Identifies singular/plural forms
- Identifies present/past tense

Spelling
- Spells words with:
  -3 to 5 letters
  -beginning/ending consonant sounds
  -short/long vowels
  -consonant/vowel digraphs
  -consonant blends
- Takes simple dictation
- Spells simple irregular words

Handwriting
- Prints upper/lower case correctly
- Uses proper letter size/spacing
- Copies printed patterns accurately

Study Skills
- Follows written directions

- Identifies alphabet by name
- Writes sequence of alphabet
- Begins use of dictionary

Mathematics

Mathematics
- Counts/writes numbers to 100
- Counts by 5s/10s to 100
- Identifies 1s and 10s place value
- Matches number to set, 0 to 20
- Memorizes addition/subtraction facts to 10
- Subtracts combinations to 10
- Recognizes ½ of whole object

Measurement
- Understands value of penny, nickel, dime, quarter, dollar
- Recognizes hour and half-hour
- Names/understands days of week and months
- Measures in inches/centimeters
- Uses cup/pint
- Compares weights using balance
- Understands temperature

Geometry
- Recognizes similar/congruent shapes
- Names basic geometric shapes
- Completes a given pattern

Application (Problem Solving)
- Solves story problems—one operation

Music

- Sings and listens for pleasure
- Plays rhythm instruments
- Learns holiday, folk, patriotic songs

Physical Education

- Ball skills—throw/catch/bat
- Uses playground equipment
- Plays organized games
- Improves coordination
- Learns roles of players in games

Reading

Readiness
- Reproduces shapes
- Uses left-to-right eye movement
- Identifies like/unlike forms
- Identifies letters

Phonics/Word Analysis
- Recognizes short vowel sounds
- Recognizes initial consonant sounds
- Recognizes ending consonant sounds
- Blends sound elements
- Reads words with short vowels

Vocabulary
- Reads color words
- Reads number words
- Reads basic sight words
- Reads own dictated stories

Comprehension
- Sequences words to form a sentence
- Follows written directions

Literature
- Listens to stories
- Uses library correctly
- Reads simple books for pleasure

Science

The study of science differs from district to district but may include all or some of the following:

- The five senses
- Animals/plants of the world
- Composition of the earth
- Sounds and how they travel
- Growth and development of the body

Social Studies

- Roles of people in the family
- Roles of people at school
- Responsibility and rules at school
- Community helpers/workers
- Understanding the neighborhood
- Appreciation of other cultures

Second-Grade Expectancies

Art

- Improves eye/hand coordination
- Creates seasonal projects

- Develops expression through art
- Works with a variety of media

Citizenship

- Develops positive attitude toward authority
- Learns leadership/followership
- Develops appreciation of American heritage
- Develops moral understanding—honesty, courtesy, consideration, respect
- Understands rights of others

Health

- Personal health/disease prevention
- Mental/social health
- Nutrition/basic food groups
- Dental health
- Safety practices

Language

Listening/Speaking
- Follows oral directions
- Retells events in sequence
- Participates in discussion
- Listens to literature
- Memorizes songs/poems
- Identifies words that rhyme
- Participates in group speaking
- Shares stories with class

Composition (Grammar/Usage/Writing)
- Writes a complete sentence
- Writes simple paragraphs
- Expresses thoughts in writing
- Capitalizes days of week/month/persons
- Uses period/question mark correctly
- Uses singular/plurals correctly
- Uses correct pronoun forms
- Uses adjectives/adverbs correctly

Spelling
- Spells words with silent consonant patterns
- Spells words with long vowel patterns
- Spells words with digraphic vowel patterns
- Identifies unstressed syllables
- Spells nouns with plural endings
- Spells verbs with past tense/progressive endings
- Takes simple sentence dictation

Handwriting
- Prints upper/lower case letters legibly
- Uses proper letter size and spacing
- Copies printed patterns accurately
- May begin cursive writing in second semester

Study Skills
- Follows written directions
- Writes sequence of alphabet from any letter
- Alphabetizes to first letter
- Identifies parts of a book

Mathematics

Basic Computation
- Counts by rote to 200

Basic Computation (continued)
- Counts by 2s to 20
- Recognizes numbers to 100
- Recognizes ordinal numbers, first-tenth
- Identifies place value 1s/10s to 99
- Adds one-digit numbers horizontally (equations)
- Adds/subtracts 2-place numbers with/without regrouping.
- Identifies odd/even numbers
- Identifies and writes fractional parts (½, ⅓, ¼)

Measurement
- Names/assigns value to penny, nickel, dime, quarter, half-dollar, dollar
- Recognizes/names quarter-hour
- Understands calendar, names/counts months
- Measures in inches, feet, yards, centimeters, meters
- Uses cup, pint, quart, pound, kilogram

Geometry
- Draws rectangle, circle, triangle, square
- Understands one, two, three dimensions

Application (Problem Solving)
- Fills in missing numbers in sequence
- Solves one-step story problems
  -addition/subtraction basic facts to 18
  -more than two addends
  -using money

Music
- Sings and listens for pleasure
- Plays rhythm instruments
- Learns holiday, folk, patriotic, children's songs

Physical Education

- Develops ball skills—throw/catch/kick/bat
- Uses playground equipment
- Plays organized games
- Develops eye/foot coordination
- Practices player roles in games

Reading

Phonics/Word Analysis
- Recognizes consonant blends
- Reads words with long vowels
- Divides compound words
- Reads consonant blends/digraphs
- Understands silent vowels/consonants
- Identifies syllables in a word
- Identifies root words

Vocabulary
- Reads basic Dolch sight words *

Comprehension
- Places three sentences in sequential order
- Recalls story details
- Analyzes feelings/motives of characters
- Identifies main idea
- Completes sentence using context clues
- Identifies sequence of events
- Draws conclusions from stories

---

* A list of basic vocabulary words that educators have used as a guide in teaching beginning language. Developed by Dolch, E., Teaching Primary Reading. Champaign, IL: Gerrard Press, 1941.

Literature
- Listens to more detailed stories
- Uses library independently
- Reads books for pleasure
- Shares books with others

Science

The study of science differs from district to district but may include all or some of the following:

Life Science
- Animals and their food chain
- Animals of long ago
- Where plants and animals live

Physical Science
- Magnets
- Heat and light
- Electricity

Earth Science
- Solar system
- Weather
- Air and water

Social Studies

- Knowledge of physical environment
- Map reading skills
- How people function in groups
  -roles within a group
  -need for rules, government
  -cooperation/decision-making
  -use of resources

- American ethnic groups
- American holidays and customs
- Current events

Third-Grade Expectancies

Art

- Works with a variety of media well
- Creates seasonal projects
- Practices expression through art

Citizenship

- Develops positive attitude toward authority
- Practices leadership/followership
- Develops appreciation of American heritage
- Develops moral understanding—honesty, courtesy, consideration, respect
- Understands and respects rights of others

Health

- Understanding of diseases—causes, prevention
- Personal health habits
- Dental health
- Safety practices—pedestrian/bicycle
- First-aid procedures
- Drugs and drug abuse

Homework

- Homework may be assigned on a regular basis and may be about ½ hour in length

- Regular homework will probably consist of learning spelling words and math computation facts

Language

Listening/Speaking
- Follows oral directions
- Retells events in sequence
- Participates in discussion
- Listens to literature
- Memorizes songs/poems
- Uses descriptive words to tell about objects
- Uses sentences with proper noun–verb agreement

Composition (Grammar/Usage/Writing)
- Completes an open-ended paragraph
- Writes three or more related sentences with proper punctuation
- Writes creative stories
- Begins writing reports in correct form
- Identifies common/proper nouns
- Identifies action verbs
- Capitalizes sentence, holidays, titles
- Uses period, question mark, exclamation mark, comma, correctly
- Uses contractions
- Uses possessive pronouns correctly

Spelling
- Spells words with:
  -Double consonant endings
  -Silent consonant patterns
  -Short vowel patterns
  -Long vowel patterns

-Digraphic vowel options
-Unexpected vowel sounds
- Identifies unstressed final syllables
- Spells noun plurals, comparative adjectives, multi-syllabic words
- Takes simple dictation

Handwriting
- Writes cursive letters in upper/lower case
- Writes using proper letter formation, letter size, and spacing
- Writes using proper slant

Study Skills
- Follows written directions
- Alphabetizes to second letter
- Uses table of contents correctly
- Uses a dictionary correctly

Mathematics

Basic Computation
- Rote counts by 5s and 10s to 200
- Recognizes/writes numbers in/out of sequence from 1 to 1000
- Knows addition/subtraction facts from 0-18
- Knows odd and even numbers from 1-10
- Identifies place value 1s, 10s, 100s, 1000s
- Memorizes basic multiplication and division facts from 0-5

Measurement
- Reads and writes dollars and cents
- Tells time to nearest 5 minutes

Measurement (continued)
- Knows time equivalents (seconds, minutes, hours, days, weeks, months, year)
- Knows measurement abbreviations (ft, cm, etc.)

Geometry
- Identifies point, line, line segment
- Identifies parts of a circle
- Understands parallel and perpendicular

Application (Problem Solving)
- Adds/subtracts 3-place numbers with/without regrouping
- Finds parts of a whole—¼, ⅓, ½
- Makes change up to $5.00
- Uses cup, pint, quart, gallon, half-gallon
- Estimates and measures length
- Solves one-step addition/subtraction word problems to 99
- Adds and subtracts money problems
- Adds and subtracts like fractions

Music
- Sings and listens for pleasure
- Plays rhythm instruments
- Sings holiday, folk, patriotic, and children's songs

Physical Education
- Uses ball skills—throw/catch/kick/bat
- Uses playground equipment
- Plays organized games
- Organizes games independently
- Develops team spirit

Reading

Phonics/Word Analysis
- Identifies initial and final consonant digraphs
- Substitutes initial blends and digraphs
- Reads "y" as consonant or vowel
- Reads "w" as consonant or vowel
- Reads and understands contractions
- Understands synonyms, antonyms, homonyms

Vocabulary
- Reads basic Dolch sight words

Comprehension
- Answers factual questions
- Identifies main ideas
- Interprets sentence/paragraph meaning
- Predicts logical outcome
- Finds main idea, locates evidence
- Interprets reactions of characters

Literature
- Listens to more detailed stories
- Uses library independently
- Reads books for pleasure
- Develops favorite characters/authors
- Shares and reports on books

Science

The study of science differs from district to district but may include all or some of the following:

Life Science
- How plants grow/produce food

- Plants and their environments
- Plant and animal relationships

Physical Science
- Chemical changes of matter
- Types of simple machines

Earth Science
- Composition and formation of the earth
- Solar system

Social Studies

- Understanding of communities, with focus on the local community
- Geography/history/government of communities
- People/cultures and their interdependence in communities
- Reading of maps, globes, graphs

Fourth-Grade Expectancies

Art

- Works well with a variety of media
- Creates seasonal projects
- Practices expression through art

Citizenship

- Develops positive attitude toward authority
- Practices leadership/followership
- Develops appreciation of American heritage

- Develops growing moral understanding—honesty, courtesy, consideration, respect
- Understands and respects rights of others

Health

- Keeping a healthy body
- Dental health
- Safety practices—pedestrian/bicycle
- Drugs and drug abuse

Homework

- Homework may be assigned on a regular basis and may be about one hour in length
- Regular homework will probably consist of learning spelling words and math computation facts
- Assignments may also be made in reading in the content areas and library books
- Research and reports, particularly in science and social studies, will be expected

Language

Listening/Speaking
- Follows oral directions
- Retells events in sequence
- Participates in discussion
- Listens to literature
- Memorizes songs/poems
- Uses descriptive words in telling stories
- Presents oral reports using complete sentences

- Listens to and summarizes information
- Uses grammar when speaking

Composition (Grammar/Usage/Writing)
- Uses common and proper nouns
- Uses a/an correctly
- Identifies adjectives
- Writes sentences with noun-verb agreement
- Uses action verbs
- Capitalizes proper nouns and initials
- Uses comma in a series of words
- Uses apostrophe for contractions
- Uses colon in time of day
- Identifies complete/incomplete sentences
- Writes reports from factual information
- Writes events in sequence
- Identifies possessive, singular/plural nouns
- Identifies the subject and predicate of a sentence
- Writes a friendly letter with correct capitalization and punctuation
- Uses contractions correctly

Spelling
- Applies spelling rules
- Spells words with long/short/silent vowel sounds
- Spells words with silent consonant patterns
- Takes dictation

Handwriting
- Practices neatness/legibility in written work
- Uses both manuscript and cursive/upper and lower case correctly
- Writes using proper letter formation, letter size, spacing, and slant
- Writes legibly from chalkboard or written page

Study Skills
- Follows written directions
- Alphabetizes to third letter
- Uses a dictionary correctly
- Uses index/table of contents
- Demonstrates use of the card catalog
- Uses telephone directory
- Writes correct book reports

Mathematics

Basic Computation
- Recognizes and writes numbers in and out of sequence to 1,000,000
- Identifies place value to 10,000
- Adds 3, 5-place number columns
- Memorizes basic multiplication/division facts through 9
- Multiplies 2- and 3-digit numbers by 1-digit number; 2-digit number by 2-digit number
- Divides 2-digit dividend by 1-digit divisor with and without remainder
- Divides 3-digit dividend by 1-digit divisor
- Identifies common fractions in numerical form
- Rounds numbers to 100 to nearest 10
- Adds and subtracts fractions
- Understands Roman numerals through 1000

Measurement
- Reads thermometer
- Knows common measurement abbreviations
- Recognizes simple equivalence (4 qt. = 1 gal.)

Geometry
- Understands radius, diameter, circumference of a circle
- Identifies sides, angles, and vertices of polygons
- Understands perimeter and area of rectangles

Application (Problem Solving)
- Makes change to $5.00
- Tells time to minute (non-digital clock)
- Measures length to ½" and ¼"
- Multiplies money by whole number
- Solves story problems with 2 or more operations
- Completes a number pattern
- Makes a bar graph

Music

- Sings and listens for pleasure
- Plays rhythm instruments
- Sings holiday, folk, patriotic, and children's songs
- May begin instrumental music

Physical Education

- Uses ball skills—throw/catch/kick/bat
- Uses playground equipment
- Plays organized games
- Organizes games independently
- Develops team spirit
- Develops strength, endurance, flexibility, and coordination
- Develops habits of good sportsmanship

Reading

Phonics/Word Analysis
- Identifies prefixes, suffixes, root words
- Reads words with vowel diphthongs
- Reads words with "R" controlled vowel
- Divides words into syllables
- Uses context clues to identify words

Vocabulary
- Expands vocabulary at grade level

Comprehension
- Summarizes written material
- Identifies cause and effect
- Applies critical analysis
- Predicts logical outcomes
- Identifies sequence of events
- Differentiates between reality and fantasy
- Reads for comprehension in the content areas, particularly science and social studies

Literature
- Enjoys more detailed stories
- Uses library independently and reads for pleasure
- Shares and reports on books

Science

The study of science differs from district to district but may include all or some of the following:

Life Science
- Study of plant physiology
- Body systems and their function

Physical Science
- Magnets and their use
- Electricity
- Study of light

Earth Science
- Management of natural resources
- Climate and weather
- Rocks, minerals, and fossils

Social Studies

- Uses maps and graphs for information
- Understands the democratic process
- Generally, fourth-grade social studies emphasizes the study of the local state, including history, geography, government, famous people, and in relation to the United States and world

Fifth-Grade Expectancies

Art

- Works well with a variety of media
- Creates seasonal projects
- Practices expression through art
- Develops an appreciation of visual art

Citizenship

- Develops positive attitudes toward authority
- Practices leadership/followership
- Develops appreciation of American heritage

- Develops moral understanding—honesty, courtesy, consideration, respect
- Understands and respects rights of others

Health

- Drugs and drug abuse, including alcohol and tobacco
- Safety practices—pedestrian/bicycle

Homework

- Homework may be assigned on a regular basis and may be about 1 hour in length
- Regular homework will probably consist of learning assigned spelling words, and doing reading in the content areas
- More independent work will be expected: reading for information, writing reports, current events

Language

Listening/Speaking
- Follows oral directions
- Retells events in sequence
- Participates in discussion
- Listens to literature
- Memorizes songs/poems/writings
- Uses descriptive words in telling stories
- Presents oral reports using complete sentences
- Listens to and summarizes information
- Uses correct grammar when speaking
- Identifies main ideas and stays on a single topic
- Listens to orally presented material and takes notes

Composition (Grammar/Usage/Writing)
- Identifies pronouns as a noun substitute
- Uses adjectives and adverbs correctly
- Recognizes incorrect double negatives
- Identifies state-of-being verbs
- Identifies and uses conjunctions
- Identifies and uses helping verbs
- Capitalizes titles of people
- Writes four types of sentences: declarative, interrogative, exclamatory, and imperative
- Writes social letters and addresses an envelope
- Understands research techniques and writes reports
- Writes complete stories with introduction, body, and conclusion
- Proofreads own material for grammatical and spelling errors
- Uses quotation marks correctly
- Uses synonyms and antonyms

Spelling
- Applies spelling rules
- Spells words with irregular consonant and vowel patterns
- Spells words with long vowel, digraph vowel, and vowel-r options
- Expands usage of prefixes and suffixes
- Takes dictation
- Develops use of the dictionary for correction of spelling errors

Handwriting
- Practices neatness and legibility in written work
- Uses both manuscript and cursive/upper and lower case correctly

- Writes using proper letter information, letter size, spacing, and slant
- Writes legibly from chalkboard or written page

Study Skills
- Follows written directions
- Alphabetizes to any letter in a word
- Uses a dictionary correctly for alphabetization, syllabication, pronunciation, and definition
- Understands and uses an encyclopedia
- Understands the use of the card catalog: author, title, subject, call number of book
- Writes correct reports on factual material

Mathematics

Basic Computation
- Identifies place value to 1,000,000
- Recognizes relationship of numerator to denominator
- Understands proper and improper fractions, mixed numbers, simplest terms, and equivalent fractions
- Adds/subtracts like fractions
- Multiplies/divides simple fractions
- Finds equivalent fractions
- Rounds numbers between 1 and 900 to nearest 100

Measurement
- Divides money by whole number
- Adds/subtracts hours and minutes
- Measures to ½" or 1 centimeter with ruler, meter, or yard stick
- Recognizes relationship of linear measures within metric system
- Measures in milliliters and liters

Geometry
  • Recognizes and names sphere, cube, cylinder, prism, pyramid

Application (Problem Solving)
  • Makes change to $10
  • Divides money by whole numbers
  • Completes a number pattern
  • Reads circle, line, and bar graphs
  • Solves one-step word problems using all operations (add, subtract, multiply, divide) with whole numbers
  • Solves two-step word problems involving addition/subtraction

Music

  • Sings and listens for pleasure
  • Plays rhythm instruments
  • May begin instrumental music
  • Sings holiday, folk, patriotic, and children's songs

Physical Education

  • Uses ball skills—throw/catch/kick/bat
  • Uses sports equipment
  • Learns the rules and concepts of organized games
  • Participates in basketball, volleyball, softball, soccer, football
  • Organizes games independently
  • Develops team spirit

Reading

Phonics/Word Analysis
- Identifies prefixes and suffixes and the way in which they alter a word
- Reads long vowels, short vowels, and "R" controlled vowels
- Identifies the base form of a verb
- Uses context clues to identify words

Vocabulary
- Expands vocabulary at grade level

Comprehension
- Places events in sequence
- Applies critical analysis
- Identifies cause and effect
- Recognizes topic sentences
- Identifies author's main idea
- Predicts logical outcomes
- Differentiates between reality and fantasy
- Reads for comprehension in the content areas
- Analyzes the feelings, traits, or motives of characters in a passage

Literature
- Enjoys more detailed stories
- Uses library independently and reads for pleasure
- Shares books and stories

Science

The study of science differs from district to district but may include all or some of the following:

Life Science
- Products and by-products of plants
- Vertebrates and invertebrates
- The human body: structure, function of cells, organs, and systems

Physical Science
- Chemical composition of elements, compounds, mixtures, solutions
- Sound as a form of energy

Earth Science
- The earth's resources: metal, fuel, soil, minerals, elements
- The oceans: plant and animal life, the effect of pollution
- The universe: solar system, galaxies, stars, orbits, gravity, and space travel

Social Studies

Generally, fifth-grade social studies emphasizes the study of the United States including:

- Geography and natural resources
- Exploration and settlers
- Founders of the nation
- Contributions of famous Americans
- Government
- Role of America in the world
- Uses of maps and graphs for information

Sixth-Grade Expectancies

Art

- Works effectively with a variety of media
- Creates seasonal projects
- Practices expression through art
- Develops an appreciation for visual arts

Citizenship

- Develops positive attitudes toward authority
- Practices leadership/followership
- Develops appreciation of American heritage
- Develops moral understanding—honesty, courtesy, consideration, respect
- Understands and respects rights of others

Health

- Drugs and drug abuse, including alcohol and tobacco
- Safety practices—pedestrian/bicycle
- Consumer health and nutrition
- Personal health

Homework

- Homework may be assigned on a regular basis and may be about 1 hour in length
- Regular homework consists of learning spelling words, reviewing computation facts, doing research, writing reports, reading in the content areas, and current events

Language

Listening/Speaking
- Follows oral directions
- Retells events in sequence
- Participates in discussion
- Listens to literature
- Memorizes songs/poems/writings
- Uses descriptive words in telling stories
- Presents oral reports using complete sentences
- Listens to and summarizes information
- Uses correct grammar when speaking
- Identifies main ideas and stays on a single topic
- Listens to orally presented material and takes notes

Composition (Grammar/Usage/Writing)
- Uses pronouns as noun substitutes
- Uses correct tense (past/present/future) of regular verbs
- Uses adverbs
- Uses state-of-being verbs
- Uses possessive pronouns correctly
- Uses helping verbs
- Capitalizes important words in titles, initials, beginning words, and parts of a letter
- Uses comma in direct address
- Uses comma to set off introductory words, i.e., yes, no, well, etc.
- Uses apostrophe for singular possession
- Underlines titles of books, magazines, newspapers
- Identifies subject and predicate
- Combines two simple sentences into a compound sentence
- Writes paragraphs with topic sentences and related details

- Writes imaginative/narrative paragraphs
- Writes business letters
- Addresses envelopes correctly
- Understands research techniques and writes reports
- Proofreads own material for grammatical and spelling errors
- Selects correct parts of speech to complete sentences

Spelling
- Applies spelling rules
- Takes dictation
- Develops use of the dictionary for correction of spelling errors
- Expands usage of words with irregular consonant and vowel patterns

Handwriting
- Practices neatness and legibility in written work
- Uses both manuscript and cursive/upper and lower case correctly
- Writes using proper letter formation, letter size, spacing, and slant
- Writes legibly from chalkboard, written page or dictation

Study Skills
- Follows written directions
- Alphabetizes to any letter in a word
- Uses a dictionary correctly for alphabetization, syllabication, pronounciation, and definition
- Understands and uses an encyclopedia
- Understands the use of the card catalog: author, title, subject, call number of book
- Uses outline format
- Writes correct reports on factual material

Mathematics

Basic Computation
- Identifies place value to tenths, hundredths, and thousandths
- Multiplies 4-digit number by 3-digit number
- Finds common multiples
- Divides any number by 2-digit divisor
- Proves division problems by multiplication
- Finds least common denominator
- Changes improper fractions to mixed numbers and vice versa
- Adds/subtracts like and unlike fractions
- Adds/subtracts mixed numbers
- Multiplies/divides proper fractions
- Multiplies/divides mixed numbers
- Adds/subtracts decimals with same place value
- Multiplies/divides decimal numerals

Measurement
- Applies linear measurement correctly and is accurate to ⅛"
- Applies liquid measurement correctly

Geometry
- Identifies parallel and perpendicular lines
- Finds the perimeter of polygons
- Finds the area of squares/rectangles
- Finds the area of a circle

Application (Problem Solving)
- Makes change correctly in any amount
- Completes more complicated number patterns
- Uses graphs to answer questions
- Computes sales tax, discounts, sale prices

- Solves two-step word problems involving multiplication and division

Music

- Sings and listens for pleasure
- Plays rhythm instruments
- Sings holiday, folk, patriotic, and children's songs
- May begin instrumental music—band/orchestra

Physical Education

- Uses ball skills—throw/catch/kick/bat
- Learns the rules and concepts of organized games
- Plays organized games—basketball, softball, volleyball, football, soccer
- Organizes games independently
- Develops team spirit
- Develops habits of good sportsmanship

Reading

Phonics/Word Analysis
- Uses context clues to identify words
- Uses word-attack skills correctly

Vocabulary
- Expands vocabulary at grade level

Comprehension
- Applies critical analysis
- Identifies cause and effect
- Recognizes topic sentences
- Identifies the author's main idea

- Predicts logical outcomes
- Differentiates between reality and fantasy
- Reads for comprehension in the content areas
- Analyzes the feelings, traits, or motives of characters in a passage
- Scans written material

Literature
- Reads full-length novels/books
- Uses library independently and reads for pleasure
- Shares books and stories

Science

The study of science differs from district to district but may include all or some of the following:

Life Science
- Interdependence of body systems
- Types of body cells
- Animal behavior
- Human growth and development

Physical Science
- Magnetic/electrical energy
- Elements, atoms, compounds, molecules

Earth Science
- Atmosphere of the earth
- Weather prediction
- Man's dependence on the environment

Social Studies

Generally, sixth-grade social studies emphasizes the study of the world and its people including:

- Geography and natural resources
- Diverse cultures
- History and explorers
- Contributions of world citizens
- Basic institutions: government, education, family, beliefs

Middle-School or Junior-High Expectancies

Beyond fifth grade, school structures begin to differ. Middle school or junior high may begin at sixth, seventh, or eighth grade and curricula will differ. It will be sufficient to look at one structure and its recommendations to get an idea of what elements may be important at this level

Since the publication of A Nation At Risk [1], the length of the school day has been carefully scrutinized. It is generally agreed that a middle-school day should consist of approximately 360 minutes. On a daily basis, the following should be included in the middle-school curriculum for one period of at least fifty minutes each: reading, literature, language arts, mathematics, science and health, history, and geography. Also included in the course of study should be visual and performing arts, physical education, and elective or exploratory courses to include a foreign language, group guidance, and computer literacy.

For more detailed information in middle school curriculum, good references include The Middle School Years [2] or Caught In The Middle [3].

High-School Expectancies

A Nation At Risk [1] also details minimum recommendations for the comprehensive high school. The commission recommended a school year of from 200 to 220 days and a school day of at least seven hours. This, however, is not what is found in general practice.

The high school curriculum should include four years of English, three years of mathematics, three years of science, three years of social studies, and one-half year of computer science. Two years of a foreign language are recommended for the college-bound youngster.

For recommendations of the high-school curriculum standards, see *Academic Preparation For College* [4], or *Model Curriculum Standards, Grades Nine Through Twelve* [5].

References

1. *A Nation At Risk.* Washington, D.C.: U.S. Government Printing Office, 1983.
2. Fenwick, J. *The Middle School Years.* San Diego, CA: Fenwick Associates, 1986.
3. *Caught In The Middle.* Sacramento, CA: California State Department of Education, 1987.
4. *Academic Preparation For College, What Students Need to Know and Be Able to Do.* New York, NY: The College Board, 1983.
5. *Model Curriculum Standards.* Sacramento, CA: California State Department of Education, 1985.

APPENDIX C:

Selected References for Parents

General Information on Choosing a School

Bedley, G. *How Do You Recognize A Good School When You Walk Into One?* Irvine, CA: People-Wise Publications, 1980.

Bedley, G. *The A B C D's of Discipline.* Irvine, CA: People-Wise Publications, 1979.

Bell, T. *Active Parent Concern.* Englewood Cliffs, NJ: Prentice-Hall, 1976.

Bushkin, M. *Parent Power.* New York, NY: Walker and Co., 1975

Good Schools: What Makes Them Work. Arlington, VA: National School Public Relations Association, 1981.

Westen, S. *Choosing a School for Your Child.* Washington, DC: U.S. Department of Education, 1989.

Guidance for Parents

Bloom, B. *All Our Children Learning: A Primer for Parents, Teachers and Other Educators.* New York, NY: McGraw-Hill Book Co., 1981.

Fields, T. *Help Your Child Achieve in School.* New York, NY: Villard Books, 1987.

52 Ways to Help Your Child Learn. Burlingame, CA: California Teachers Association and the National Education Association. (Booklet)

How To Help Your Child Learn. Washington, DC: National Education Association of the United States, 1960. (Booklet)

Johnson, B. *Helping Your Child Achieve in School.* Novato, CA: Arena Press, 1985.

Kaban, B. and Shapiro, B. "How to raise a competent child." *Harvard Magazine,* July-Aug 1975. (Article)

Research

WHAT WORKS: Research About Teaching and Learning. Washington, DC: United States Department of Education, 1987.

Private School Information

Handbook of Private Schools. Boston, MA: Porter Sargent Publishing, Inc. (Published annually)

Private Schools of the United States. Shelton, CT: Market Data Retrieval, 1985-6.

Information is also available by writing:

American Association of Christian Schools
P.O. Box 1088
Fairfax, VA 22030

Association of Christian International Schools
P.O. Box 4097
Whittier, CA 90607

Council for American Private Education
1625 Eye Street, N.W.
Washington, DC 20006

National Independent Private Schools Association
120 W. Church Street
Frederick, MD 21701

Self-Education

Lines, P. "An Overview of Home Instruction," *Phi Delta Kappan.* March 1987.

Wade, T. *The Home School Manual.* Auburn, CA: Gazelle Publications, 1986.

Booklets and Inexpensive Materials

Cavazos, L. *Educating Our Children: Parents & Schools Together.* Washington, DC: U.S. Government Printing Office, 1989. (Booklet)

Light, W. *A Parent Guide to Grade Retention.* Novato, CA: Academic Therapy Publications, 1981. (Booklet)

Looking In On Your School. Chicago, IL: The National PTA, 1982. (Booklet)

What to Look For When You Visit Your Child's School. Washington, DC: National Education Association. (Booklet)

Your Child and Testing. Pueblo, CO: National Institute of Education, Consumer Information Center. (Booklet)

The following booklets are available from the U.S. Government Printing Office, at minimal cost, by writing:

Consumer Information Center-L
P.O. Box 100
Pueblo, CO 81002

Becoming a Nation of Readers: What Parents Can Do. 29 pp.

Books for Children. 19 pp.

Help Your Child Become a Good Reader. 5 pp.

Help Your Child Do Better in School. 5 pp.

Help Your Child Improve in Test-Taking. 5 pp.

Help Your Child Learn Math. 7 pp.

Help Your Child Learn to Write Well. 5 pp.

The following booklets are available from the National School Public Relations Association by writing:

NSPRA
1801 N. Moore St.
Arlington, VA 22209

Good Teachers: What To Look For. 15 pp.

Helping Your Child Learn. 15 pp.

A Parent's Guide to Standardized Aptitude and Achievement Testing. 15 pp.

Teaming Up On School Discipline. 15 pp.

That First Day At School. 15 pp.

The following booklets are available from:
Channing L. Bete Co.
200 State Road
South Deerfield, MA 01373

About Self-Esteem. 15 pp.

How to Help Your Child Learn. (in Spanish)

Your Child Entering School. 15 pp.

Your Child's Potential To Learn. 16 pp.

The following booklets and materials (some in Spanish) for parents are available from the National Congress of Parents and Teachers by writing:

National PTA
700 N. Rush Street
Chicago, IL 60611

Discipline: A Parent's Guide

Help Your Young Child Become a Good Reader

Help Your Young Child Learn at Home

Looking In On Your School: A Workbook for Improving Public Education

Plain Talk About Tests

A series of booklets for parents, mostly related to the area of reading, are available from the International Reading Association by writing for a complete list:

IRA
800 Barksdale Road
P.O. Box 8139
Neward, DE 19711

A series of booklets for parents is available from the National Educational Association by writing:

NEA Professional Library
P.O. Box 509
West Haven, CT 06516

Glossary of Selected Educational Terms

Achievement—
The level at which a student is able to perform in a particular area, such as reading or math

Active Learning—
The direct involvement of the learner in an educational activity

ADA—
Average Daily Attendance. The average number of students in attendance at the school adjusted for absenses

AFDC—
Aid to Families with Dependent Children. Money provided to families who do not earn enough to support their children, the basis on which some federal money is allocated to schools.

Aptitude—
The ability of a student to do work or perform a task

Articulation—
Joining together sequential parts of an educational program, as from one grade to another

At Risk—
A term used to describe a group of students who are predicted to be in danger of dropping out

Basic Skills—
The language arts; reading, writing, spelling, and mathematics.

Bilingual Education—
A classroom organization that enables teaching the curriculum in two languages

Chapter I (formerly called Title I)—
Federal program that allocates funds to the schools for the purpose of helping disadvantaged learners or at-risk students

Cognitive Domain—
The intellectual behaviors of the student; knowledge

Compensatory Education—
Educational programs, such as Head Start or Chapter I, designed to make up for elements lacking in a child's education or home background

Competency Test—
A test used to determine if a student has achieved a predetermined level of skill in an area

Computer Assisted Learning—
Programs designed to be presented on the computer, resulting in learning similar to that received in more conventional ways

Cooperative Learning—
A teaching technique that assigns students to specific tasks that are accomplished only through cooperation of two or more students for one answer or problem solution

Continuum—
A series of skills organized by levels of difficulty

Core Curriculum—
The basic course of study

Curriculum—
The organization of the body of material that will be studied

Departmentalization—
Organization of the curriculum broken down by subject areas

Essentialist—
An educational program or school organization that stresses the basic skills

ESL (English as a Second Language)—
An instructional program that teaches non-English speaking children to speak English

Gifted—
Children in the above-average intelligence range

Handicapped—
A physical or mental condition that limits the student's participation in normal school activities

Head Start—
A prekindergarten compensatory education program that seeks to develop readiness skills in disadvantaged children

Individualized Instruction—
Organization of the classroom that permits each child to be instructed or learn at his/her own pace or learning style

Interdistrict Choice—
A plan allowing a parent to select a school outside of the district attendance area.

Intradistrict Choice—
A plan allowing a parent to select any school within a district.

I.Q.—
A term used to describe a student's ability to do school work. An average child has a score of "100"

Language Minority—
Students whose primary language is other than English

Learning Disability—
A handicap that inhibits or prevents instruction in a normal manner

Magnet School—
A school that features a particular area of interest, such as science, math, computers, language, etc., which is used to draw students

Manipulatives—
Learning tools or concrete objects that can be handled for the purpose of learning from them

Middle School—
An organizational plan, less formal than the traditional Jr. High, which seeks to bridge the gap between elementary and high school usually during grades six, seven, and eight

Mission (School)—
A statement of the school's philosophy or goals

Open Enrollment—A plan whereby parents are allowed to enroll their child in any school in which there is room.

Passive Learning—
Learning that is presented to the student rather than involving the student in the discovery process

Phonetic Approach—
A word attack method of reading that depends on sounding out a word using specific clues

Proficiency—
To show mastery in the application of a skill

Readiness—
A stage of development that allows the child to begin more formal learning because basic skills which enable learning are in place

Remediation—
A process of giving special attention and reteaching to skills that have been taught but not sufficiently mastered

Self-Esteem—
The feelings that a student has for her/himself, relates to her/his ability to do work

Standardized Test—
A test that measures a student against similar students in a norm group, locally, statewide, or nationally

Structured—
A classroom organization in which more formal procedures govern the teaching and learning activities

Team Teaching—
A cooperative method of planning for, teaching, and evaluating a group of students by more than one teacher

Time On Task—
The time when students are involved directly in the learning process rather than the housekeeping activities in a classroom

Title I—
See Chapter I

Tuition Tax Credit—
Tax relief granted to parents who send their child to a private school that requires tuition.

Ungraded—
A school organization that dispenses with grade levels, and groups students by their progress toward specific goals

Unstructured—
The opposite of structured

Vouchers—
A paper payment, issued by local, state, or federal authorities that allows a parent to select and pay for a school of their choice.

Year-Round School—
An organization of the school year that staggers vacation times so that the school is in session for more regular periods of time, for instance, "45-15" or 45 days of study and 15 days of vacation.

Index

Ability, 39
Academic achievement, 85, 119, 211
Acceptance, 68
Active learning, 27, 211
Activities, non-educational, 130
ADA, 211
Adjustment, 68
AFDC, 211
After school programs, 112
Alcohol, 10
Anxiety, 69
Application process, 149
Aptitude, 211
Articulation, 212
Assembly area, 107
Assessment, of student progress, 74
At risk, 212

Attendance, 141
  areas of, 149
Attention, 75
Attitude, 68
Aural learner, 44
Average learner, 68
Average ability, 41

Basic skills, 2, 212
Basics program, 30
Behavior, student, 92, 110
Bilingual education, 212
Books, on education, 7
Bulletin boards, 131

Chapter I, 212
Child care, 20, 112
Citizenship, 59
Class size, 106
Classroom, observation, 129

Cognitive ability, 34
Cognitive domain, 212
Compensatory education, 212
Competency test, 212
Computer, 12
Computer-assisted learning, 212
Continuous progress, 30
Continuum, 213
Contract learning, 33
Conversation, with child, 140
Cooperation, 70
Cooperative learning, 213
Core curriculum, 212
Curriculum, 83, 213

Decision making, 62
Departmentalization, 213
Developmental concept, 33
Developmental factors, 66
Dignity, individual, 122
Disabilities, 48
Discipline, 92, 132
Diversity, of students, 57
Drugs, 10

Education, continuing, 89
Educational terms, 211
Effective schools, 81
   checklist, 132, 151
Effective teacher, 116

Emotional needs, of child, 140
ESL, 52, 213
Essentialist, 213
Ethnic balance, 112
Expectancies
   Kindergarten, 164
   1st grade, 169
   2nd grade, 173
   3rd grade, 179
   4th grade, 184
   5th grade, 190
   6th grade, 197
   high school, 203
   middle school, 203
Expectations, 75, 91
   grade level, 111
   growth, 155
   learning, 155
   student, 119

Family structure, 11
Financial support, 104
Forgetting, 69
Future, of school, 112

Gifted, 47, 213
Grade structure, 22
Grouping, student, 132
Growth characteristics
   Kindergarten, 156
   1st grade, 157
   2nd grade, 158

3rd grade, 159
4th grade, 160
5th grade, 161
6th grade, 161
7th grade, 162
8th grade, 163
Growth, 66
    philosophy of, 122

Handicapped, 213
Head Start, 213
Health, 66
Home schooling, 17
Home–school relationships,
    94, 120
Homework, 75, 86
    policy, 111

I.Q. (see Intelligence)
Immigrants, 4
Individuality, 66, 122
Individualized instruction,
    214
Information
    gathering, 124
    written, 125
Instructional process, 132
Instructional strategies, 90,
    119
Instructional time, 92, 120
Intelligence, 34, 40, 69, 214
Interdistrict choice, 214
Interest, in child, 141

Intergroup relations, 99
Intradistrict choice, 214
Involvement, of students, 97

Kinesthetic learner, 44

Language minority, 50, 214
Leadership, administrative,
    83
Learning
    disability, 214
    lifelike, 75
    process, 70
    styles, 44, 70
    triangle, 136
Library, 107
Location, of school, 116
Love, of children, 121

Magnet concept, 34
Magnet program, 113, 214
Manipulatives, 214
Mathematics, at home, 143
Meaningful experiences, 76
Memorizing, 71
Middle school, 214
Mission, school, 83, 215
Modeling, 78
Montessori program, 33
Morale, student, 121
Motivation, 78

Ongoing education, 55
Open classroom, 31
Open enrollment, 215

Parents
    as teachers, 37, 66
    attitude toward school, 147
    role, 136
Passive learning, 27, 215
Patterns, 72
Performance ability, 34
Personal considerations, 115
Personality, 52
Phonetic approach, 215
Physical needs, of child, 139
Physical plant, 106
Playground, 107
Policies
    behavior, 110
    homework, 111
    promotion, 111
    pupil placement, 111
    retention, 111
    school, 108
Positive reinforcement, 132
Practice, 73
Praise, 70
Principal, 83
Private schools, 17, 149
Problem solving, 140
Proficiency, 215
Promotion, policy, 111

Psychological information, 68
PTA, 128
Punishment, 73
Pupil placement, policy, 111

Readiness, 67, 215
Reading, at home, 142
Recitation, 78
References, for parents, 205
Relations with others, 58
Remediation, 215
Repetition, 73
Reputation, of school, 113
Responsibility, 24, 99
    at home, 145
    for behavior, 58
Retention, policy, 111
Rewards, 73

School climate, 96
School mission, 83, 108, 119
Secretary, school, 128
Self-concept, 42, 61, 70
Self-esteem, 97, 215
Sense of humor, teacher, 121
Special needs, 47
Special programs, 114
Staff, instructional, 87
    movement of, 87
    paraprofessionals, 89
    variety of, 87

Standardized tests, 40, 215
Structure, 74, 215
Student progress, 93, 120
Student work, 86
Study skills, 78, 144
Success, 78

Teacher, effective, 116
Teaching methodology, 74
Team teaching, 34, 216
Technology, 12
Television, 8, 145
Tension, 69
Testing, 94, 102
Time on task, 74, 216

Title IX, 3
Transportation, 114
Tuition tax credit, 216
Tutoring, 74

Ungraded, 216
Unstructured, 31, 216

Visiting a school, 127
Visual lerner, 44
Volunteers, 89
Vouchers, 216

Writing, at home, 143

Year-round school, 34, 216